PENGUIN BOOKS S

Marcus Grant was born in [illegible] 1945. He went to school in Inverness, Edinburgh and Paris, before qualifying in English at Pembroke College, Cambridge. Having already published and broadcast a number of short stories and poems, he went on to lecture in English Literature, first in Chichester and then back in Cambridge. In 1973 the Alcohol Education Centre was founded to co-ordinate national training in alcoholism and, shifting career completely, Marcus Grant was appointed its first Director. Since then he has written and edited numerous books on alcohol problems, especially on issues to do with prevention and education. He has an honorary appointment with the Institute of Psychiatry, University of London, and is Chairman of the Education Section of the International Council on Alcohol and Addictions. Over the years, he has advised on alcohol and drug policy in many parts of the world, including North and South America, Australia, the Western Pacific and Europe. He now works with the World Health Organization in Geneva on their global programme on alcohol-related problems. Marcus Grant also writes novels under the pseudonym of Tom Gilchrist. He is married to an archaeologist, and they have two daughters, Rachel and Josie. Marcus Grant still describes himself as a moderate drinker.

MARCUS GRANT

SAME AGAIN

A GUIDE TO SAFER DRINKING

PENGUIN BOOKS

Penguin Books Ltd, Harmondsworth, Middlesex, England
Viking Penguin Inc., 40 West 23rd Street, New York, New York 10010, U.S.A.
Penguin Books Australia Ltd, Ringwood, Victoria, Australia
Penguin Books Canada Ltd, 2801 John Street, Markham, Ontario, Canada L3R 1B4
Penguin Books (N.Z.) Ltd, 182–190 Wairau Road, Auckland 10, New Zealand

First published 1984

Made and printed in Great Britain by
Cox & Wyman, Reading, Ltd
Set in Photina by Northumberland Press Ltd,
Gateshead, Tyne & Wear

For Beryl, after so many words

CONTENTS

INTRODUCTION

This book is written for everybody who is interested in their own drinking or in the drinking of somebody close to them. Alcohol is popular, and deservedly so. For most people, most of the time, drinking is simply part of a way of life, a source of harmless pleasure.

On the other hand, drinking too much causes problems. Not just hangovers, but accidents – at home, at work and on the roads. In the longer term, there can be serious damage to mental and physical health, to family relationships, to work prospects and to self-esteem.

Nobody who drinks even a small amount is immune to the problems which alcohol can cause, but it is possible to learn to drink in ways which cut down the risks. It is not just a matter of how much and how often, although these are important factors. It is also a matter of developing particular drinking habits, of learning a particular drinking style.

If it is your own drinking that you are concerned about, you should be able to use this book as a self-help guide. It will help you to analyse your present drinking patterns and will suggest ways in which you can achieve and then maintain drinking practices that are more to your liking.

If you are concerned about the drinking of somebody close to you, then this book is intended to help you, as well as to help the drinker. Whoever it is – your husband or wife, a friend, a colleague, another member of your family – it can be very difficult to do anything about this problem without seeming to be interfering. There is also the risk that you could not only fail to help but, in attempting to do so, sacrifice your relationship with your friend. This book will suggest ways of approaching other people about their drinking and ways of coping with the difficulties you may encounter.

Some people may have alcohol problems which are so severe and so intractable that they require immediate professional help. This book is not really written for them, although it does include some information on how to go about seeking such help.

There is, however, a whole world of people between those who only drink a very little and those who have already done themselves serious damage. It is a world of ordinary drinkers, it is a world of regular drinkers, and it is a world of occasional heavy drinkers. It is for this large world of people that this book has been written. Its purpose is not to make abstainers of you all. Far from it. Its purpose is to enable you to drink more safely, without sacrificing the pleasure.

'Same again' might be the call of the alcohol addict reaching for yet another bottle. It might be the call of the doctor in the accident unit as yet another drunken driver's victim is wheeled in for emergency treatment. It might be the despairing call of the abandoned wife waiting for her husband to return in a violent temper from the pub. Or of the social worker looking at the sad spectacle of a family driven into neglect by the drinking of the parents. It could be all those, and many more.

But 'same again' could also be the simple certainty that moderate drinking will indeed bring relaxation, pleasure and a sense of well-being. That is what you can be calling for when you cry, 'Same again'. All the pleasure and none of the pain.

1. DRINKING – THE EVERYDAY PLEASURE

It is all too easy to take drinking for granted. In most countries in the world alcohol is becoming more and more readily available. While only a minority of people actually drink it literally every day, many drink so regularly that it would be unusual for them to go a whole week without touching alcohol in some form. For most people, drinking is a pleasurable social activity, something which they often do as part of other social activities, such as meeting friends for a chat or a meal, or to aid relaxation at home or in the pub. Since, for most people most of the time, alcohol adds to pleasure and causes no problems, it is hardly surprising that it simply becomes one of the better parts of everyday life. In that sense, it is like a lot of other commodities that make life easier in one way or another.

But alcohol is not just another commodity, like chocolate or cornflakes. It is a drug – probably the most commonly taken drug in the world. Like other drugs, it is best used to benefit those who consume it. But, like other drugs, it can also cause problems when it is misused. That is why society has laws to regulate the supply of alcohol through controls over its production and distribution. In the end, however, it is up to each individual to learn how best to use alcohol so as to reap the maximum benefits from it while avoiding the problems caused by excessive or inappropriate consumption.

Learning to drink is not necessarily as easy as it sounds. It has to do with quantity – how much you drink; with frequency – how often you drink; and, perhaps most important of all, with your style of drinking. While it is possible to formulate relatively hard and fast rules for quantity and frequency, *how* you actually drink on any particular occasion, or during any particular phase of your life, is likely to relate to all sorts of external factors – where you are drinking, who you are drinking with, why you are drinking and what you expect to do next – as well as to internal factors, such as whether you are feeling happy or depressed, confident or anxious, lively or tired and whether you are physically in good shape or not. The consequences of your drinking are likely to be affected by just the same sorts of variables. If you are feeling tired and anxious and you then have a few drinks with your boss before driving home through busy traffic, the end result may be very different from the result of your consuming exactly the same amount of alcohol while sitting in front of your favourite television programme with your family.

Used well, alcohol certainly can enhance life. It makes you feel better in a thousand unquantifiable ways. Unfortunately, used badly, it can cause a great deal of harm, both to the drinker and to those others – family, friends and colleagues – who surround the drinker. Sometimes it may even be the unknown victim of a drunken driver who suffers.

Alcohol, in other words, is a problematic substance and drinking is a problematic activity. That does not mean that it is wrong or that it ought to be avoided. It is perfectly possible to argue, both from a common-sense and from a strictly economic point of view, that alcohol confers more benefits than costs to society. To see drinking as problematic is simply to call attention to the fact that it cannot be taken for granted. It is an activity with potential complications and dangers and you need to give it careful thought and come to some specific decisions in order to avoid ending up among the statistics for liver cirrhosis, mental illness or traffic accidents.

In a way, alcohol is like the motor car and drinking is like driving. Each brings many benefits to society, but at some cost. Each is a complicated activity, requiring many different decisions. Each is permitted only once people have passed some legal minimum age. Each is a common, everyday activity, bringing simple pleasure to many, easing the difficulties of life and, almost casually, maiming and killing a small proportion of people in the meantime. Yet the rules of driving have to be learned carefully and methodically in order to cut these casualties down as far as possible, while the rules of drinking are mostly just habits you pick up here and there, from your parents, your friends, your colleagues and from behaviour you see on television and in alcohol advertising.

It is only comparatively recently that an attempt has been made to resolve that anomaly. Doctors and others concerned with treating alcoholics have begun to point out that excessive drinking emerges from normal drinking and that there is no clear-cut demarcation line between the two. If you want to avoid alcohol problems, they are saying, then it is a bit too late to wait until you are already addicted. You have to begin before the troubles ever start. Just as with dieting – where it is better to stay slim all along rather than to go to fat, start on a crash diet, go to fat again and so on – so it is better to maintain a safe and healthy drinking style rather than to alternate between periods of heavy drinking and periods of enforced total abstinence.

Thus it is important to consider simultaneously the quantity, the frequency and the style of the drinking episodes. Only a combination of these three different elements will enable you to obtain a clear picture of your own drinking behaviour. Since much of what follows in this book will be based on the idea that you need to have a clear understanding of what your drinking is really like (and not just a vague sense of it being mostly no particular trouble), then it is important to spend some time clarifying each of these three elements – quantity, frequency and drinking style.

It may be that it is somebody else's drinking which is troubling you, rather than your own. If so, exactly the same thing is true. You are unlikely to be able to be of any help to that person, or to assist him or her towards self-help, until you know exactly what it is that you are trying to change. Although you may feel that you are all too familiar with the problems caused by a particular set of drinking habits (your own or somebody else's), it is essential at this stage to take nothing for granted and to try to obtain as objective a view as you can of quantity, frequency and style of drinking.

Quantity

There are three main kinds of alcoholic drinks – beers, wines and spirits. When considering the quantity being drunk, it is important to distinguish between the alcohol as such (ethyl alcohol, to give it its proper name) and the simple volume of liquid, together with all the other substances (known as congeners) which go to give each beverage its distinctive taste. The number of these congeners can vary from a mere handful in the case of a very light distilled spirit, such as vodka, to several hundred in the case of a heavy red wine, port or brandy. Although it is possible that different people will react differently to particular congeners and although it is certainly true that the drinks with the largest number of congeners are those which are most likely to produce hangovers, it is the alcohol which is the most important active ingredient and the one which is relevant in estimating quantity.

Beer is sold in pubs in half-pint and pint measures. It is sold in bottles of a third of a pint, half a pint, one pint and one quart. Of these, the half-pint bottle accounts for about 80 per cent of all bottle sales. Some imported lagers are sold in bottles of a third of a litre, which is just slightly more than half a pint. Beer is also sold in two standard size cans. These are the ten-ounce or half-pint can and the sixteen-ounce or forty-five-centilitre can. The larger size of can now accounts for more than half the sales of canned beer.

There is no standard strength for beer. The average strength is 3.7 per cent alcohol by volume. Most keg beers are within one or two decimal points of this strength, but lager has a wider range of strengths, from about 3 to 5 per cent alcohol by volume, with some of the special strength lagers even reaching 8 per cent. Barley wines can be as strong as 10 per cent.

For those interested in the dietary side of drinking, it is worth noting that the average pint of beer contains between 170 and 200 calories, although a number of diet lagers with a much lower calorie content are now produced.

Most wine is sold by the bottle. The most common size of bottle is either seventy or seventy-five centilitres, depending upon its country of origin. This is approximately equivalent to a pint. The other common size for bottles of wine is one litre, although larger bottles of one and a half or two litres also exist. Wine is also made available to the domestic market in half bottles (35 cl) and a variety of other containers, including the so-called 'bag in a box' containers of three or five litres, which are estimated to account for about 10 per cent of total wine sales in Britain. Pubs and wine bars often serve wine by the glass. There is no standard size for such glasses: most contain about 12.5 centilitres, although some are up to 50 per cent larger. For home consumption, it is generally safe to estimate that an ordinary bottle of wine contains seven glasses and a litre bottle ten glasses.

The average strength of table wine is about 10 per cent alcohol by volume. Generally, red wines tend to be stronger, say 11–12½ per cent alcohol by volume, and white wines can sometimes contain as little as 8½ per cent alcohol by volume.

A glass of dry wine contains about 80 calories and a glass of sweet wine up to 110 calories. To estimate the total number of calories in a bottle, multiply by seven for an ordinary bottle and ten for a litre.

Sherry and port are known as fortified wines. They are produced by adding a spirit (usually brandy) to a wine base. Most aperitifs, such as vermouth, are produced by similar methods but are further altered by adding various herbs for their distinctive flavours. There is a certain amount of variation in strength between sherry and port, with port tending to be slightly stronger, and between different aperitifs. On average, however, something like 19 per cent alcohol by volume seems to be a reasonable estimate of the strength of fortified wines. The size of the bottles is usually the same as an ordinary wine bottle, although litre bottles are now becoming more common. An average glass of sherry or port is usually about seven centilitres, which contains from about 80 calories (for dry sherry) up to 140 calories (for sweet port).

Of the spirits, the ones which are most commonly drunk in Britain are whisky, gin, vodka, brandy and rum. They are sold in bottles containing twenty-six and two thirds fluid ounces. Litre bottles of spirits are usually only available in duty-free shops. A single measure or 'tot' of spirits in a pub contains one sixth of a gill in England, Wales and Northern Ireland and one fifth of a gill in Scotland. There are thirty-two single measures in a standard bottle of spirits.

The strength of spirits is fixed by law and is indicated on the label by what is called 'proof' level. This expression comes from a method of assessing the strength of spirits which has now, happily, ceased to be used. The method involved adding a mixture of water and spirit to gunpowder and then increasing the proportion of spirit to the point when the gunpowder could explode. The spirit was then deemed to have been proved.

Proof level is shown on the label by a number which is followed by the sign °. In Britain, whisky, gin, brandy and rum are all 70° proof and vodka is 65°, as are one or two cheap whiskies.

The proof level is *not* the same as the percentage of alcohol by volume in the drink. In the rest of Europe, where a different proofing system is used, the figure shown *is* a simple metric equivalent of the percentage of alcohol: a bottle of French brandy at 40° is actually 40 per cent alcohol by volume and is the equivalent of 70° proof by the British system. The European system is called Gay Lussac, after its inventor. A further complication is that the Americans have yet another separate proofing system, which shows the proof level as double the Gay Lussac figure.

To give you a sense of what the equivalents are between these proofing systems, it is worth studying this table:

British proof	**Gay Lussac** *(European proof)*	**American proof**	**% Alcohol**
175	100	200	100
88	50	100	50
80	45	90	45
75	43	86	43
70	40	80	40
65	37	74	37

The number of calories in a single measure of spirits depends to some extent upon the particular drink chosen, but an average of about 55 calories seems reasonable. Remember, however, that spirits are often drunk with mixers, such as tonic, ginger ale or coke, which will add to the calorie count. Also, many people buy double measures in pubs and are accustomed to pouring even larger measures when drinking spirits at home.

There are, of course, other alcoholic drinks which are not included in this list. Cider, for example, can for most purposes be thought of as the equivalent to beer. Liqueurs are sometimes even stronger than other distilled spirits and can contain as much as 55 per cent alcohol by volume. Some of the stronger aperitifs can contain about 25 per cent alcohol by volume, and tonic wines have an average strength of about 20 per cent alcohol by volume.

All this is, of course, terribly confusing. Different sizes of bottles, different sizes of glasses, different levels of alcohol by volume, lack of standardization and variations within beverage categories all make it extremely difficult to estimate exactly how much alcohol you have drunk on any one occasion. It is, remember, the alcohol, the most significant active ingredient in all these drinks, which must be measured. The law, recognizing how difficult it is to produce accurate figures in any other way, looks to the proportion of alcohol in your bloodstream as the only reliable measure of intoxication.

At this stage, however, it is only quantity of alcohol consumed that is being estimated, rather than intoxication, which refers to the effects of alcohol in the short term and which will be examined later. Bearing in mind, therefore, all the different figures quoted above, it is obviously extremely difficult for any reasonable person, even with a pocket calculator ready throughout an evening's drinking, to keep an accurate running total of how much he has had to drink, particularly if he is switching from one beverage to another.

The concept of a 'standard drink' may be of more immediate help. You have seen the different strengths of different kinds of drinks and also the different measures in which they are generally available. As it happens, the most commonly available measures of the most common drinks all contain *roughly* the same amount of alcohol. Using the metric system of measurement for the alcohol, half a pint of beer contains 1.05 centilitres of alcohol, a single measure of spirits contains 0.94 centilitres (slightly more in Scotland, where one fifth of a gill is the standard measure), a glass of wine contains 1.04 centilitres and a glass of fortified wine about 1.12 centilitres.

In other words, half a pint of beer, a single tot of spirits, a glass of wine or a glass of sherry all contain approximately one centilitre of alcohol. This can be used as a convenient measure for a standard drink.

It is important to stress that this is a rough guideline only, but it is accurate enough for most self-monitoring purposes, and is certainly a great improvement on having no idea at all how much you have been drinking. Using the standard drink as your basic unit of measurement, it is easy enough to construct a rating system for most commonly drunk quantities.

1 standard drink	½ pint beer (lager, cider) 1 single tot of spirits 1 glass of wine 1 glass of sherry, port, aperitif
2 standard drinks	1 pint beer Double measure of spirits ½ pint special strength lager
4 standard drinks	1 pint special strength lager
7 standard drinks	1 ordinary bottle of wine
10 standard drinks	1 litre bottle of wine
12 standard drinks	1 bottle of sherry, port or aperitif
15 standard drinks	½ bottle of spirits
30 standard drinks	1 bottle of spirits

In estimating the quantity you have drunk on any particular occasion or over some particular period of time, this standard drink rating system will probably prove to be the most convenient way of reaching a reasonably accurate total.

Frequency

It is not just how much you drink that is important, but also how often you drink. Although there are bound to be variations in your drinking, depending upon the time of year, holidays, Christmas, birthdays and so on, most people do have a fairly regular drinking pattern, which provides a context for any variations that do occur. Again, although this section is written in terms of looking at the frequency of your own drinking, the same principles apply if it is the drinking of somebody else that you are trying to assess. Quantity by itself is certainly an important factor, but even quite modest drinkers occasionally have a particularly heavy session, which need not be unduly significant. What happens when you look at quantity and frequency together is that a *pattern of drinking* begins to emerge.

In the next section, when you look at drinking styles, that pattern will begin to take on particular colours. What is happening now is that you are sketching in its outlines.

People who drink less frequently than once a week are unlikely to have problems related to alcohol, unless their consumption levels when they do drink are very high indeed. However, even if you drink only once or twice a week on average, it is important to try to link that frequency of consumption to particular levels of consumption in order to get a sense of your drinking pattern. If you usually have a drink three or four times a week or if you think you probably have a drink most days, then it is even more important to be as accurate as possible at this stage.

Just because it is so easy to take drinking for granted, it is sometimes difficult to remember when you had a drink unless you approach the question quite systematically. People who are asked to give an estimate of their drinking during an average week consistently underestimate both the quantity and the frequency of their drinking. A good way to begin is to try working out how often (and how much) you actually drank last week. Begin with yesterday and work backwards one day at a time. Think your way through the whole day: morning, lunchtime, afternoon, mealtimes, evening. Work out how many drinks you had on each occasion. Fill in the diary chart on the next page, using the standard drink as your basic scoring unit. Remember, half a pint of beer equals a glass of wine equals a single measure of spirits.

Here is an example of a diary chart which somebody has filled in for the previous week's drinking.

	Beer	Spirits	Wine	Sherry, etc.	TOTAL
Monday	*2*				*2*
Tuesday					
Wednesday	*1*	*4*			*5*
Thursday					
Friday	*4*		*2*		*6*
Saturday	*4*	*4*			*8*
Sunday			*3*	*2*	*5*
WEEKLY TOTAL					*26*

Not a particularly heavy drinker, you might think. But there were only two days on which some alcohol was not consumed.

The week's drinking must have looked something like this: on Monday, a pint of beer at lunchtime; on Tuesday, nothing; on Wednesday, half a pint on the way home and then a couple of large whiskies while watching television; Thursday, nothing; on Friday, two glasses of wine at lunchtime and two pints in the pub in the evening; Saturday evening in the pub again, drinking a couple of pints and a couple of double whiskies; and

Sunday, at lunchtime, a sherry before, three glasses of wine with, and a port after.

Now try working out your total for yourself.

	Beer	Spirits	Wine	Sherry, etc.	TOTAL
Monday					
Tuesday					
Wednesday					
Thursday					
Friday					
Saturday					
Sunday					
WEEKLY TOTAL					

If you are trying to fill the chart in for somebody else, you will need to go through the same process. Work backwards, a day at a time, trying to make sure that you do not miss anything out. There is no point in underestimating or overestimating drinking. Try to be as accurate as possible.

Above all, do not make excuses about how it was not a typical week. Some people are for ever explaining away days of particularly heavy drinking on the grounds that it was a 'special occasion'. If you were to add up all the special occasions in the year, you might find that they were not quite so special after all. Family birthdays, birthdays in the office, parties at friends' houses, anniversaries, club dinners, local celebrations, Christmas, New Year, Easter, holidays, official functions – for some people the list seems endless. If you entertain or are entertained a lot, then that for you is part of your drinking pattern and it is important that you take it into account when estimating the quantity and frequency of your drinking.

If, on looking at your week's total, you feel that it really is not a fair estimate of your average drinking pattern, then use the same system to keep a diary of your actual drinking for the next week or two. Do not try to remember back beyond last week, because it has been shown that people's estimates become markedly less accurate beyond a single week. If you do keep a diary for a week or two, see if the simple act of noting down each drink as you have it has any impact upon the amount you drink or the way you feel about your drinking. A certain amount of self-consciousness about your drinking pattern is one of the most important prerequisites for effective self-monitoring. It helps you take this everyday activity just a little bit less for granted.

Drinking Style

It must already be apparent to you how much more difficult it is than it seems at first sight to achieve an accurate picture of what a particular drinking pattern (your own or somebody else's) is really like. It seems as if you need to be a human computer to work out quantity and to have superhuman powers of memory to work out frequency. Compared to estimating drinking style, however, both of these other factors are quite simple.

In thinking about drinking style, there are two different influences at work which combine to determine what sort of drinking it is that is going on. One of those is the drinking *occasion* – that is to say, the particular set of circumstances in which any single drinking episode is taking place. The other is something which only becomes apparent over time – namely, the drinking *habits* of the individual. It is the correlation between your drinking habits and the drinking occasions in which you find yourself that creates your particular drinking style.

You could say that there are as many drinking styles as there are individuals. Up to a point, that is perfectly true. Certainly, the main purpose of this book is to help individuals to work out, achieve and maintain the particular drinking style which best suits them.

Inevitably, however, there are some general guidelines within which individual variations can be better understood. Read these five short case histories. They are all based upon the everyday drinking experiences of ordinary drinkers. Perhaps none of them exactly corresponds to your own drinking style, but try to look for elements with which you feel sympathetic. If it is somebody else's drinking that concerns you, try to suspend judgement for the time being and just look for some general similarities between that person and some of the behaviour patterns that emerge in these case histories. Notice as you read these accounts that they are not from people who believe that they have problems with their drinking. They are all reasonably well satisfied with their drinking styles. Ask yourself whether you share that sense of satisfaction.

BILL (aged 26; unmarried; double-glazing contractor)

'It's not that I'd rip anybody off, you understand, but there's a fair bit of money to be made in my trade if you know how to go about it and if you're prepared to put in a bit of hard graft. Which I am. So, put it like this, I'm not short of a few bob.

'There's no point having a bit of money unless you enjoy it, is there? I take decent holidays – you know, Canaries, Malta, even the Caribbean once. I have a decent motor – a Lotus, less than two years old. And I like to have a drink.

'Not every day. Don't get me wrong. Most days, in fact, I don't touch a drop. Just weekends. That's all. I like to spend weekends with my friends. And I like to have a few drinks with them. There's no harm in that, is there? I'm careful not to take the Lotus if I know I'm going to be having a few. I'm not stupid. I don't want to lose my licence.

'Typical weekend? Well, Friday I'll get back to the flat about six or half past, have a good wash-up and then round to the local. There's a few of us gather there regularly on a Friday at that time. Have a couple of jars and moan about the week. Tell each other stories about how hard up we all are. Complain about the health and safety inspectors and swap tips on how to pull a fast one on them. That sort of thing.

'Then I'll meet the girlfriend about eight. I've got this new

girl now – Deborah – she's really clever, you know, doing A-levels at a sixth form college. And she's a real smasher, you know what I mean, to look at and . . . well, when she gets going. I've never had an intelligent girlfriend before. She's all right, though.

'So we go out for a meal then. Bottle of wine, drinks before and after. Then we go back to my place. We usually have a bit more to drink there too, I suppose. She still lives with her parents, so she can't stay the night. I usually put her in a taxi at about one or two. I don't like that bit at all. I'm trying to persuade her to move away from home.

'Then Saturday, well, there's always a bit of shopping to do in the morning, then lunchtime I usually meet the same crowd I see on Friday evenings. We have a few drinks before going off to the match together. Not that the club's doing so well this year, but loyalty counts for something, doesn't it?

'Deborah and I usually have a party or something on a Saturday night. She likes dancing, you know, does all these Jane Fonda classes. She's got a good body and she knows how to move it. It's difficult to estimate how much you drink at a party, isn't it? I mean, you don't tend to stick to the same stuff, do you? Sometimes it's wine, then the next thing it's vodka. I don't take anything else, by the way, pills or anything, I don't approve of that. No, I've no idea how many I'd have at an average party, but I'll tell you this – I'd certainly not be fit to drive home.

'I don't get up till lunchtime Sundays and I go straight down to the pub then. Usual crowd. Then the afternoon kind of slips by and, often as not, Deborah comes round to my place in the evening. I enjoy my weekends. Why not? I work hard enough the rest of the week. I deserve a bit of a break, don't I?'

JENNIFER (aged 43; unmarried; senior secretary)

'Actually, I prefer working in a larger firm, because you tend to meet more people. Small firms can be terribly claustrophobic. The company I work for now is an ideal size. There's about fifty of us in the office. Then there's the factory, of course, but we're quite separate from them. I'm personal secretary to Mr Billings, the export sales manager. He travels overseas a great deal, of course, so that means that I have quite

a lot of responsibility, especially when he's away. I like to think that I'm sufficiently experienced to know exactly what I'm doing.

'There is a staff canteen, but I don't particularly like it. Three or four of us – not all senior secretaries, there's one of the office juniors as well – like to go out to the local wine bar for lunch. It only opened up last year, but we've become quite the regulars now. They do a very good lasagne and we usually share a bottle of wine between us. Sometimes two, if it's a special occasion or if there's no particular reason to rush back to our typewriters.

'It's true that I didn't use to drink at lunchtime at all, but I can't say that I notice it interfering with my work. If anything, it makes me a bit more tolerant of some of the stupid mistakes of others.

'In fact, I've developed something of a taste for wine. I don't mean that I drink vast quantities of it. Indeed, I've become extremely discriminating. I've joined one of those wine clubs, you know the sort of thing. You have to buy a whole case at a time, of course, but I find I've got into the rather pleasant habit of opening a bottle when I have my evening meal and then finishing it off later in front of the television. Very quiet and civilized. I live alone, of course, and it'd never even occur to me to have a second bottle in an evening. But, to be frank, it's been a great source of quiet pleasure to me. I do get a bit lonely from time to time and sometimes in the past that used to depress me so that I couldn't seem to sleep properly. Now, with my bottle of wine and four channels on the television, I'm really cosy for the evening. And I never have any difficulty getting to sleep, not now. I like to keep myself to myself, and there's nothing wrong with that, you know. I lead a well-ordered life and I don't interfere with other people's pleasures. There's not many that can say as much.'

DEBORAH (aged 17; unmarried; student)

'No, my parents don't approve of my drinking. But then my parents don't approve of lots of things about me. My clothes, my music, my boyfriend, my whole way of life. Come to think of it, I don't much approve of my parents.

'I don't want you to think that I drink just because they disapprove, though. I know there are some of my friends who do things just to shock their parents. I think that's really childish. And I'm not

a child. I'm old enough to make my own mind up about what I like and what I don't like. One of the things I like is alcohol. Frankly, I expect it does me a lot less harm than all those cigarettes my dad smokes or all those Valium my mum takes just to keep herself going from one day to the next.

'I actually enjoy drinking because it's something I always do with friends. I don't suppose I've ever had a drink alone. I can't imagine wanting one. But when you're with friends, you know, meeting them in a pub or a club or something, I mean, you'd feel stupid if you weren't drinking. Anyway, it makes things more fun, it really does, that's obvious, otherwise it wouldn't be sold there, would it?

'I have this boyfriend – the one my parents disapprove of – who's a bit older than me. I find boys of my own age very immature. Bill – that's his name – is really very sure of things, very sure of what he wants out of life. I admire that. He's not especially well educated, but that doesn't matter so much nowadays, does it? I think my parents are real snobs about that kind of thing, I mean, Bill's got a lot more natural intelligence than either of them, for example.

'He takes me out a lot at weekends, Bill does, and we tend to drink quite a bit then. Well, we're with people most of the time, like I said. Or, when we're alone together, well, drinking can be a very intimate thing, can't it? All that stuff about it interfering with the performance just isn't true, at least not for Bill and me. Sorry, does that shock you?

'During the week I have the odd drink with friends from college. Just in the evenings. Never more than one or two, though, or seldom. I mean, I've got my essays to write and so on, haven't I? I like having a good time, but I mean to get good A-level results too. I want to go to university. I mean to make the most of life. And that's what I'm doing now.

'It's true, of course, that I sometimes have a bit too much to drink. I feel really lousy the next day and vow that I'll never touch another drop. That resolution usually lasts for no more than twenty-four hours, but that's the way with all good resolutions, isn't it? I mean, it would be really boring to live a wholly virtuous life. I think so, anyway. You won't catch me being bored with life. The last thing I want to do is to end up like my parents.'

MICHAEL (aged 39; married; export sales manager)

'After a time, you find that all the airports merge together into a kind of continuous feeling of being marooned outside space and time. It doesn't matter if it's Frankfurt or Sydney or KL. If you're stuck there at some godforsaken hour of the day or night because of – what do they always say? – "operational reasons", then there's nothing much you feel like doing except having a drink.

'I exaggerate, of course, but it's surprising how effective alcohol is at helping one cope with the sort of life I have to lead. For a start, it's part of the daily grind of business. And why not? Goodness knows, one works hard enough for it, those interminable meetings, those impossible deadlines, those estimates you could drive a coach and four through. And, worst of all, having to be able to make quick decisions, there and then, without being able to run the new information through the computer, without being able to check out Brazilian contract law with one's tame legal beaver. It's a continual headache. And alcohol helps to ease it.

'I wouldn't like to tell you the number of times that a good lunch with a couple of decent wines and a bottle of armagnac has smoothed over all the wrinkles and ruffled feathers left after a hard morning round the negotiating table. Or the number of times that a quiet dinner with a key figure from the other side has enabled me to close a deal that looked impossible only an hour or two earlier. All that's to do with alcohol, don't tell me it's not. It's the effect it has, certainly, encouraging confidences, but it's also part of the ritual, part of the way of showing people they're special.

'After all, that's true enough with women too, isn't it? And I've had my share of experiences on that score as well. It's inevitable, travelling the world as I do, that one meets people – I mean women – here and there and, of course, there's never enough time to go through all the usual business of getting to know somebody. Well, alcohol helps one short-circuit a lot of that.

'So, business and pleasure, alcohol's bound up with both. But I wouldn't like you to get the impression that my life's a continual round of business lunches and intimate suppers for two in my hotel suite. As I said at the beginning, a lot of my time's taken up with waiting. Waiting in airports, waiting in hotels, waiting in other people's offices. It's

inevitable and I'm not complaining. Or not much. And alcohol's very important on these occasions. It helps to kill time. It helps to take the edge off one's anxiety or one's frustration.

'No, you're right, I've said nothing about my home life. That's interesting, isn't it? Well, for a start, I'm away more than I'm home. We don't have any children and we've never had tests of any sort in order to see whose fault that is. Maybe it's better that way, since I don't suppose I'd make much of a father. Does that sound bitter? I don't mean it to.

'Anyway, you'd be surprised how often my work intrudes on my home life too. We have a smart home and Harriet's an excellent cook, really excellent. It impresses a prospective client more if you can offer them dinner at your home rather than in a restaurant, no matter how expensive. That's especially true for visitors from overseas. They love to see how typical Englishmen live. Typical? Little do they know. Well, the drink does rather tend to flow on those occasions of course. Which means it's around the rest of the time as well. From the company's point of view, it's a good investment. It works well. You've no idea how charming Harriet and I can be, especially after we've had a few drinks.'

HARRIET (aged 35; married; housewife)

'It really sounds self-indulgent, doesn't it, for me to complain about my way of life? Many people would say I have everything I could possibly want. Financial security, a beautiful home, my own car, independence. Of course, they'd say, Michael's away a lot, but that's not necessarily a bad thing for a relationship. And not having children makes you even more of a free agent. Oh yes, they say wistfully, how much I envy you your independence.

'But I wonder whether I don't simply have too much independence. I mean, what do you do with it, when you've got it? What do I do? I get involved with charity work, which I'm sure is all terribly worthy. I see my friends, which is all very pleasant. I've had – I can tell you this – the odd affair, which is all rather exciting. But when all's said and done, I find myself wondering what it's all for? What's the point? Where now? Is that it, for the next twenty years, more charity work, the same friends and fewer lovers? Is that all there is to life?

'Drinking is just part of the lifestyle. When Michael's home,

there are often clients round in the evening. Fat foreigners who pinch my bottom when Michael's not looking. And sometimes when he is. I don't think he minds, provided he clinches the deal or whatever he wants out of them. I don't think I mind, actually. It helps to prove to me that I still exist.

'It's just always around, the drink. And it's so much a part of my social scene. Come round for drinks, people say. Drop in for a quick gin. Is it too early? It's never too early. Well, perhaps just another one. Same again.

'Oh, I know, I need to snap out of it. But that's easier said than done. After all, what's in it for me if I change my way of life? I might moan about how things are just now, but who's to say they wouldn't seem a great deal worse if I . . . well, whatever? I don't even know if I sincerely regret not having a child or having given up my job. I used to sell advertising space in the local newspaper. When I remember that dreadful daily routine. Or when I see the even worse routine of those friends of mine who've got children – all those nappies and then all those adolescent problems. No, thank you. I may complain about my lot but, when all's said and done, I don't think I can honestly say that I want to change it.'

Drinking Habits and Drinking Occasions

These five cases each show distinct drinking styles. At this stage, the point is not to decide whether you think they are good (optimizing the benefits of alcohol) or bad (dangerous, or potentially dangerous) but rather to notice the factors that distinguish the different drinking styles from each other. It is not sufficient to point to the obvious personality differences between the five individuals. Their personalities certainly do have an effect on the way they drink, but that is part of a larger issue to do with the whole system of values that is implied in each description of the way in which they, as individuals, relate to the world. But by looking closely at their drinking habits and how these habits operate on particular drinking occasions, it will be possible to come to a better understanding of the range of different factors you have to take into account when trying to understand somebody's drinking style.

A habit, if you like, is a consistent, linked series of

occasions in which the same sort of processes occur. You will have noticed that the five individuals whose cases appear above were all describing more or less habitual processes. Phrases like *'I usually meet the same crowd'*, *'something I always do with friends'*, *'I wouldn't like to tell you the number of times'* and *'come round for drinks, people say'* occur again and again in their accounts of their drinking lives. The sense of repeated patterns of drinking is central to the theme of this book. Remember the title – *Same Again*. Later, special attention will be devoted to how you can change the pattern of drinking if it is, for some reason, unsatisfactory. At this stage, however, the crucial first step is to understand it.

Another important point to emerge from these case histories is how people's drinking styles interlock with each other. Of course, in these cases, the relationships between the individuals make that clearer. Boyfriend and girlfriend, husband and wife, boss and secretary: as their lives touch and influence each other, so their drinking styles are influenced too. This interlocking of drinking styles is something which it is easy to forget. Sometimes, if you want to change the way you drink, the only way to achieve it may be to change the people you drink with. At this stage, however, the basic point to remember is that it is almost always going to be inadequate to look at an individual's drinking style in isolation. It is invariably going to be more helpful to see that drinking in the context of the drinking styles of those other people who surround and influence that individual.

Disentangling habit and occasion involves trying to isolate all the different factors that go to make up an individual's drinking style. It may be useful to think of these factors in terms of a series of alternatives. Some of these alternatives have to do with those issues of quantity and frequency which were discussed in more detail earlier. Here are a few either/or's:

Just one or two drinks/More than a couple of drinks

This is obviously a very important variable. Notice, for example, how on a Friday night Bill would have 'a couple of jars' with his friends, but then go out for a meal with Deborah and have 'a bottle of wine, drinks before and after'. In his mind different rules clearly applied to these two separate occasions, especially since, when meeting the same friends the next day they would have 'a few drinks' (i.e. presumably more than a couple) before going off to the match.

Jennifer, by contrast, claims that 'it'd never even occur to me to have a second bottle in an evening', as if such an idea really shocked her, although, of course, a single bottle of wine contains seven standard drinks.

Michael's quantity threshold is probably quite a lot higher than either Bill's or Jennifer's. He describes lunches 'with a couple of decent wines and a bottle of armagnac' and dinners at home with clients when 'the drink does rather tend to flow'.

The point here is simply that for different people on different occasions the question of how many drinks are consumed will be an important part of their drinking style. Bear in mind that some people seem to set their limits consistently low (or high) while others vary them according to the circumstances in which the drinking is taking place.

Always the same beverage/Range of different beverages

In view of the difficulties in estimating total alcohol consumption across a range of different beverages, there is some relevance in looking at whether people stick to a particular favourite drink or switch between different beverages. Jennifer, for example, explains that she has 'developed something of a taste for wine' and indeed it seems that she drinks nothing else.

Bill, by contrast, admits that he is unable to estimate his total average consumption at a party precisely because he drinks a range of different beverages. 'Sometimes it's wine,' he says, 'then the next thing it's vodka.' Another issue that is relevant here is, of course, whether the drink comes in a standard measure or is simply poured out as it comes from the bottle, as is doubtless the case with the vodka at Bill's party or all the drink in Michael and Harriet's house.

Again, bear in mind that people will sometimes stick to one particular beverage for one sort of occasion, but may switch to another beverage for a different occasion. You may feel it is appropriate to drink a pint of beer if you are in the pub with the local rugby fifteen but prefer to accept a glass of sweet sherry if you are visiting your maiden aunt on Boxing Day.

Most days of the week/Only at weekends

The last two alternatives dealt with the area of *quantity*, but it is important to remember that *frequency* exerts an equally powerful influence over drinking style. Somebody who always has a glass of wine with lunch and another glass of wine with dinner every single day will actually end up drinking less than somebody who never drinks during the week but goes out and has four pints of beer on Friday and Saturday night.

Harriet, for example, tells us that 'drinking is just part of my lifestyle', and Jennifer, describing her lunchtime visits to the local wine bar, admits that 'we've become quite the regulars now'. Similarly, while Deborah obviously drinks most at weekends with Bill (who claims that he does not drink during the week), she also notes that 'during the week I have the odd drink with friends from college'.

It is, in fact, the interface between quantity and frequency that is the most telling variable in assessing drinking styles. It is even possible to see this when looking at the drinking styles of whole nations. The French, for example, seldom drink so much that they are intoxicated, but the amount they generally tipple during each day means that many of them are probably never strictly speaking alcohol-free; whereas the Finns, who drink scarcely at all during the working week, often drink themselves insensible at private parties at the weekends. While these national stereotypes can sometimes be misleading in that they do not reflect the true variety of drinking styles in a country, they are useful for showing how impressive the differences can be. Nobody would be likely to confuse the drinking styles of an average Frenchman and an average Finn. They are, in a sense, worlds apart, even though the most important difference between them is something as basic as quantity/frequency.

During the day/Only in the evening

There certainly are times of the day when it is thought to be more appropriate to have a drink than at others. This is reflected in the licensing laws but also relates to other, stronger taboos than simple legal sanctions. A man weaving a slightly tipsy path along the pavement at eight o'clock in the evening would probably arouse a tolerant smile in the average passer-by, while the reaction would be much more hostile if the scene took place at eight o'clock in the morning.

Many people are wary of those who regularly have a drink at lunchtime and most people would be very suspicious of somebody who arrived at work in the morning smelling of drink. During the week, for example, Deborah says that she will have a drink 'just in the evenings' while Harriet's 'Is it too early? It's never too early' sound like a facetious justification for the total suspension of any self-restraint on her drinking.

In very broad terms it is probably true that the earlier in the day somebody starts drinking, the greater their total consumption for that day is likely to be. A drink during the morning could easily be followed by drinking at lunchtime and then again in the evening. Consumption on each drinking occasion might well not be excessive, but a drinking style which involves regular consumption throughout the day might well be one which should give some cause for alarm, since such frequency of drinking would be likely to have a multiplying effect upon quantity.

Early morning drinking is often believed to represent one of the crucial warning signs that somebody has developed a very real problem with their drinking. This is because it can be used as a means of restoring a blood alcohol level which has dropped during the hours of sleep, thus avoiding the onset of withdrawal symptoms, such as uncontrollably trembling hands, which are signs of alcohol dependence. The old 'hair of the dog' remedy for hangovers really operates on the same principle and is simply a way of taking another fix to prevent physical and emotional discomfort.

During working hours/During leisure time

When people drink is an important factor in determining their drinking style, but it is not just the hour of the day that has to be borne in mind. It is also important to understand whether the drinker sees the activity of drinking as something which is essentially a leisure pursuit or whether it is seen as being compatible with (or even in some cases an integral part of) the working day.

Michael is in no doubt about that. 'It's part of the daily grind of business', he claims and cites useful lunches 'after a hard morning round the negotiating table' to support his case. There are situations where drinking is even more closely enshrined in business practice: contracts are ritually sealed with a drink; formal toasts are made at official functions.

Some people, on the other hand, are likely to be less sure of their ground than Michael. Jennifer, for example, feels a need to justify her lunchtime drinking by claiming that 'if anything, it makes me a bit more tolerant' and asserting that it does not interfere with her work. Although Deborah only drinks in the evenings during the week, she is careful to limit her consumption strictly, since she intends 'to get good A-level results too'. She seems particularly anxious to separate her leisure time, during which she drinks quite a lot, from her work time, during which her consumption is modest. Her boyfriend Bill, who does not drink during the week but drinks heavily at the weekend, takes that principle one stage further.

Harriet, who does not have objectively defined work commitments and sees her future in terms of 'more charity work, the same friends and fewer lovers', clearly has difficulty in drawing any boundaries around her drinking. 'It's just always around', she explains, somewhat ingenuously.

Strictly speaking, there is no doubt that drinking does produce measurable changes in behaviour and in mental functioning. In terms of work performance, quite small quantities of alcohol will reduce concentration, increase reaction time, blur reflexes and decrease problem-solving skills. That is why most countries have drinking and driving laws – some of the same skills are required to drive efficiently as are required to work efficiently. Some employers, however, are prepared to tolerate levels of intoxication which would certainly be unacceptable on the highways. This is especially true, as in Michael's case, when drinking to entertain is actually part of the job and where the employee is judged more on flair and on sudden triumphs than on steady consistent performance.

In assessing drinking style, therefore, it is especially important to look at the relationship between the drinking and the working day; to see if the drinking is integrated into the work or if it is kept strictly apart from it. Does the work actively encourage drinking or is the drinking something an individual does despite the fact that it is clearly inappropriate? If drinking is confined to leisure time, is it because it is seen as a main source of pleasure in itself or because it is associated with other sociable leisure activities? These are the sort of questions which need to be answered in order to understand this particular variable in somebody's drinking style.

Paying the market price/Having access to free or cheap drink

The price of alcohol has an important effect upon the amount people consume. Even relatively small changes in price – those imposed each year on Budget Day, for example – do produce changes in total consumption, although these are often relatively short lived. Larger reductions in price – situations where people have access to cheap or even free drink – can, however, create problems. It is probable – though not invariably so – that people who can have it free or at substantially reduced rates will drink more than those who pay the full price. It has even been suggested that people for whom drinking is particularly important will deliberately choose jobs where alcohol is readily available. Certainly, barmen have very high rates of those diseases associated with heavy drinking.

Looking at the five cases set out earlier, it is clearly Michael and Harriet whose alcohol supply is subsidized in this way. Since Michael's company actually provides stocks of different beverages so as to enable him to entertain clients at his home, it is likely that they never actually buy any drink themselves for home consumption. 'It's just always around', says Harriet; and Michael, acknowledging the way this benefit extends from its actual purpose to become a perk of the job, explains that 'from the company's point of view, it's a good investment'. When he is away from home, it is likely that most of Michael's drinking is on his own or somebody else's expense account. Even when he does pay for it himself when waiting in an airport, he is probably able to take advantage of duty-free rates.

It is perhaps a natural human characteristic to want to take the maximum advantage of benefits that are offered. Alcohol is a commodity which gives pleasure for a certain sum of money; it seems both understandable and rational to seize any opportunity to obtain that pleasure for nothing. However, it is a very special commodity, and it is worth pausing to ask whether there may not be limits beyond which the financial gain (illusory in any case, if you are drinking more than you would otherwise have done) or the added pleasure are outweighed by the dangers which follow excessive consumption. If free or cheap alcohol is a privilege, then it is certainly open to abuse, if only because, as will be discussed later in this book, alcohol is an addictive substance and those who are accustomed to taking quite a lot of it are likely to need to continue to do so.

This question is particularly important to an assessment of somebody's drinking style because free or cheap drink may gradually, imperceptibly, take over a person's life. At first, it seems a legitimate subject for self-satisfaction, for boasting, even for exploitation; then, subtly, it becomes more and more important, not as a symbol of success or trust, but as an end in itself. How much you pay for something may often be the best regulation on your consumption. If you pay nothing or very little, then it is all too easy for the consumption to lose its self-regulatory restraints and to run away with itself before you are aware that it has done so. A steady round of entertaining, official functions, fully-stocked hotel minibars and free in-flight drinks may seem part of a sophisticated, jet-setting lifestyle. It may also be concealing the possibility that, without you even noticing it was happening, your drinking has slipped out of control.

Drinking in pubs or restaurants/Drinking at home

The location of the drinking occasion is related both to the question of quantity of alcohol consumed and to its degree of integration into the working day. There are, of course, many different places where drinking can occur. The alternatives shown in the heading to this section, which contrasts drinking in pubs or restaurants to drinking at home, is only a shorthand for the whole range and ignores many possible alternative drinking venues. Drinking can also take place in clubs (where different licensing laws apply), in the open air (at picnics, or in parks, where no supervision of any kind is generally available), while travelling (by air, rail or sea, when alcohol may be purchased at duty-free rates), or in many other circumstances. Basically, however, there are two factors which have to be borne in mind. Firstly, is there any kind of formal or informal supervision present? Secondly, are standard measures used for the alcohol which is provided? Generally, both the use of standard measures and the presence of supervision will have a moderating effect upon consumption; without standard measures or supervision people will tend to drink with much less restraint.

Bill and Deborah begin drinking in a restaurant on a Friday night with their 'bottle of wine, drinks before and after' but then they go back to his flat and 'usually have a bit more to drink there too'. Even Jennifer, who seems to have a strong sense of self-discipline, actually drinks quite a lot more at home in the evening (a whole bottle of wine, which equals seven standard drinks) than at lunchtime in the wine bar (one, or sometimes two bottles shared between four people). Michael, travelling the world, seems accustomed to drinking by himself 'in airports, waiting in hotels, waiting in other people's offices' and probably takes little notice of exactly how much he consumes on those occasions. Even so, simply because it involves other people serving him with the drink, it may be less than when he is trying to impress an overseas client with his generosity as a host. His wife, Harriet, who rarely seems to drink except in her own or other people's private houses, probably has a very hazy idea of how much alcohol she drinks, either on a single occasion or during an average week.

The question you should ask is whether your drinking style actually obscures your ability to undertake a realistic self-assessment of your drinking. If you cannot assess what your drinking is like, then it is going to be that much more difficult to take the further step towards self-monitoring. If a drinking location has rules (to do with the way alcohol is served and with the kinds of behaviour that are tolerated) then people choosing to drink there will expect to stay within the limits of these rules. The Brewers' Society, for example, talks about the 'therapeutic value' of the

British pub and sees it, in its way, as an instrument of moderation, since good landlords are unlikely to turn a blind eye to excessively rowdy or dangerous drunken behaviour. It is known that one of the most important factors in distinguishing those occupations which have higher than average rates of alcohol problems is their relative freedom from supervision.

Most people's drinking style is likely to involve both drinking in a pub or restaurant and drinking at home. It is certainly worth looking at this question of the location of your drinking, particularly in relation to the presence of standard measures and of supervision, and plotting out whether there is a pattern which, for example, tends to associate heavier drinking episodes with particular drinking locations where these constraints are weaker or completely absent.

Drinking in public/Drinking in private

This is an extension of the previous alternative. It is not quite the same thing as the simple location, since your home could sometimes be quite a public arena – when you are throwing a party for all your friends, for example – while a restaurant could be quite private if you are tucked away discreetly at a corner table with somebody who is close to you. A public park can sometimes be very private and a private dinner party can sometimes be surprisingly public. Similarly, drinking itself can be seen as either a public or a private pleasure.

For Jennifer, for example, her solitary bottle of wine each evening has become 'a great source of private pleasure'. Notice, however, that while Deborah is opposed to solitary drinking (a topic discussed at greater length below) and says, 'I don't suppose I've ever had a drink alone. I can't imagine wanting one,' she does see drinking as having a very private side to it. Referring to her relationship to Bill, she says that 'drinking can be a very intimate thing'. Michael, rather less romantically, describes how alcohol facilitates his sexual conquests overseas.

Harriet, on the other hand, describes alcohol as 'so much part of my social scene', and Bill, speaking for a large percentage of the population, explains that he likes to spend time with his friends and 'to have a few drinks with them'.

There is, as in so many of these alternatives, not just a simple choice between opposites, but a whole range of intermediate options as well. It is best to see most of the alternatives described here in terms of two extreme positions on a meter, say zero and a hundred, with all the other numbers in between. Few people will be at absolute zero and few at the top of the dial. Most will be somewhere in between, the point varying somewhat from week to week, month to month, or year to year. You are likely to find that some of your drinking is done in public, some in private, and some in circumstances that share characteristics of both public and private. Again, it is important to see what sort of pattern emerges and to notice if particular aspects of your drinking behaviour, such as heavier consumption than usual, are associated with particular contexts.

It may not always be obvious how these mechanisms are at work. The relationship between drinking and sexual behaviour, whatever Deborah may claim for herself and Bill, tends to be one in which desire increases as performance wanes. On the other hand, some people may need to experience the disinhibiting effects of alcohol before they are prepared to commit themselves to a sexual encounter in the first place. The part that drinking plays in the intimate theatre of either a casual or a permanent sexual relationship is therefore something that may prove to be an important aspect of your drinking style.

Public drinking occasions can exert all sorts of unanticipated pressures too. Despite the moderating influence of a genial barman, somebody who finds himself caught up in a large group of friends, all of whom insist upon buying rounds, may find that he ends up drinking a great deal more than he had intended at the beginning of the evening. The wish to conform to what you think are the dominant norms of behaviour can lead you to do things which might otherwise be quite alien to your character. While these pressures can be present in a private situation, they are likely to be especially powerful when the drinking is taking place more in the public eye. On the other hand, some public drinking occasions have strong taboos against drunkenness (say, a Garden Party at Buckingham Palace, to choose an extreme example) and the very visible nature of the drinking would be likely to promote a cautious approach to the quantity of alcohol consumed, even though the drinkers were not paying directly for what they were drinking.

Drinking alone/Drinking with friends

Solitary drinking is often quoted as an early sign of alcoholism. Like the old myth that talking to yourself is the first sign of madness, it is actually a gross simplification and is certainly not *in itself* necessarily a significant factor at all. It is worth remembering that it is the overall drinking style that is important. If somebody who lives alone and leads a quiet social life habitually has one can of beer at home each evening while watching television and scarcely ever drinks on any other occasion, then a traditional response, based upon the old-fashioned 'Test Yourself for Alcoholism' type of quizzes, might be that this is a very worrying pattern of drinking, since it was almost all solitary. If, however, the total quantity consumed is taken into account, it is clear that, although this individual habitually drinks alone, he drinks so little that he must certainly be classified as a light drinker at very low risk.

Similarly, if somebody who generally drinks rather more, say four drinks each evening, but invariably does his drinking with his wife, finds that he is alone on a particular evening each week because his wife has joined a local consumers' group, it is quite likely that he will continue to drink the amount that he is accustomed to, even though she is not with him. In those circumstances, it is not the fact of drinking alone that is important, but rather that he has become so accustomed to substantial levels of consumption that he wants to maintain his drinking level even when the circumstances in which he finds himself have changed.

It is important, in other words, to look at someone's solitary drinking habits in the context of the rest of his drinking style and in the context of his level of consumption, before coming to a hasty conclusion. He may be no more in need of drying out than somebody who sings in the bath is in need of a strait jacket.

There are, of course, aspects of solitary drinking which should give legitimate cause for concern. When you are drinking alone, there are no external controls of any kind, except the physical limit of your total alcohol supply. Thus, the potential for high levels of consumption and for accidents as a result of drunkenness are both increased. That may be why solitary drinking has come to be seen as a danger sign. If somebody is doing most of their drinking alone, then it is especially important to make sure that the actual quantity consumed does not gradually and inexorably increase over time.

Jennifer, who lives alone, seems aware of this problem. 'It'd never even occur to me to have a second bottle in an evening,' she declares. The point has already been made that a whole bottle of wine is quite a lot to drink regularly, whether or not that drinking is solitary. It may be that, since she leads what she calls 'a well-ordered life', her own self-control will be sufficient to keep her drinking at its present level. On the other hand, as she grows increasingly used to drinking at that level, she may find that it does not have the same effect upon her that it used to have. This is called 'tolerance' and might lead to her opening that fateful second bottle of wine, as she seeks to achieve the same feelings that she used to achieve when she started drinking regularly at her present level.

The other regular solitary drinker, Michael, is in a rather different position. His drinking is closely related to the circumstances in which he finds himself. Waiting in an airport lounge (or in a hotel room) by himself, he confesses, 'There's nothing much you feel like doing except having a drink.' Boredom, therefore, and lack of normal pastimes, may provoke drinking which would not otherwise occur. Later in this book the question of finding alternative activities to drinking during such periods will be discussed, since some people use boredom as an excuse for really heavy drinking. The more Michael travels, the more of a problem this is likely to be, even though he may well prefer to think of it as a problem to do with boredom rather than a problem to do with drinking.

Michael's wife Harriet does not actually say whether she drinks alone or not. If she does, however, then that might well be a case where the fact of solitary drinking, in addition to all the other aspects of her drinking style, could suggest that she was using alcohol for its drug effect, to treat her anxiety and depression. While alcohol can indeed be used, and legitimately used, for its drug effects, a situation like Harriet's, where her low mental state appears to be a relatively permanent and irreducible part of her, and where she is not seeking any other means to alleviate it, is one in which solitary drinking is indeed a sign of real danger.

It is important to look at the context within which any solitary drinking occurs. Is it a relatively isolated phenomenon or is it the most common drinking situation for that individual? Is it associated with particularly high levels of consumption or with increasing consumption (even at a lower level than might otherwise seem noteworthy)? Is it associated with a chronic low mental state? And, finally, is it something which the drinker is actually trying to conceal from other people? Of all the situations discussed here, the most worrying would be one in which somebody was drinking alone and also trying to hide their drinking. If they are trying to hide it, it can only be because they are aware that there is something wrong with it. And if they know that, but are continuing to drink despite it, then drinking has become, for them, unhealthily important.

Drinking when you're up/Drinking when you're down

In looking at the question of solitary drinking, the importance of the mood you are in when drinking emerged as a factor of some importance. Harriet's solitary drinking was seen as being more loaded with potential danger than Jennifer's precisely because Harriet seemed to lack Jennifer's self-control and to be more prone to a generally depressed outlook on life.

Unlike some of the previous variables, the mood you are in when you drink may be difficult for you to understand properly. So far, the variables have been matters of fact – the where, when, with whom and how much of your drinking. Now it is a question of interpretation. It is, if you like, a question of why. This can be an elusive aspect of your drinking style; if it is somebody else's drinking style rather than your own that is troubling you, it is likely to be particularly difficult to answer this question. Nevertheless, if a pattern is there, it is worth spending some time and effort trying to see it.

Alcohol is used at both ends of the spectrum: 'Let's celebrate – let's have a drink' is an example of the sort of phrase that accompanies a drinking episode when the drinkers are feeling happy or elated; 'I've had enough – I need a drink' is an example of the opposite. All sorts of moods can be used as reasons for having a drink – feeling tired, feeling excited, feeling cosy, feeling ill at ease, feeling satisfied, dissatisfied, proud, ashamed, confident, nervous, nostalgic, anticipatory . . . the list is endless. Drinking in response to any of these moods is not in itself necessarily good or bad. What is important, in terms of understanding your drinking style, is simply to understand whether there are particular moods which seem to act like triggers for you, moods in which you habitually find yourself feeling like having a drink.

Drinking to change your mood/Drinking to reinforce your mood

If there is a particular mood, or range of moods, that seem to be associated with drinking for you, the next question to ask is whether, in choosing to drink, you are trying to change that mood or to intensify it. Experience shows that alcohol is probably a great deal better at reinforcing moods than changing them, but that does not necessarily mean that people are always aware of that.

Jennifer, for example, suggests that it might, at least in part, be to make her feel less lonely that she drinks in the evenings. And when Harriet describes how she feels when Michael's overseas clients make sexual advances to her ('It helps to prove to me that I still exist,' she says), she might just as well be talking about her drinking. These are examples of changing moods. Deborah, by contrast, sees the role of drink as a reinforcer. 'It makes things more fun . . . that's obvious,' she says, referring to social drinking at pubs and clubs.

Is it coincidental that it is the three women who have referred, either directly or indirectly, to the relationship between alcohol and their emotional state? This could be either because emotions are more important determinants of personal and interpersonal life for women than for men, or, perhaps more likely, because men are less prepared to talk about such matters than women are. Perhaps Bill and Michael would do well to look a little more closely at how they *feel* when they start drinking and what they expect it to do for them.

Drinking for a purpose/Drinking for its own sake

Later in this book the short- and long-term effects of alcohol will be discussed in more detail. Apart from slaking thirst, however, the most obvious reason for taking a drink is to achieve whatever effects you are seeking. Sometimes these are subjective effects (such as changing or reinforcing your mood, as discussed in the last section), and sometimes they are effects upon others. It may be helpful to look at this question in terms of whether the drinking is seen as an end in itself, a simple source of subjective pleasure, or whether it has some other purpose.

Bill, for example, obviously likes drinking for its own sake. Indeed he uses it to reward himself. 'I deserve a bit of a break, don't I?' he asks rhetorically, as the main justification for his week-end drinking sprees. His girlfriend Deborah is in a much more ambiguous position. On one level she drinks because it is part of friendship, both in a general sense and in terms of her relationship with Bill. On another level, however, she admits that she is also drinking in order to avoid feeling stupid in situations where other people are drinking. Indeed, for Deborah, drinking is an important part of the statement she wants to make about herself, who she is and what sort of values she holds. 'It would be really boring,' she says, 'to lead a wholly virtuous life.' For Deborah, her drinking is one of the ways she distinguishes herself from her parents.

Much more simply, Jennifer uses alcohol to help her sleep. Michael, the most manipulative of all, certainly uses alcohol to achieve specific objectives. He uses it as an instrument of conquest, as a weapon, as a way of imposing his will upon others. That is apparent both in terms of his sexual conquests when abroad ('alcohol helps short-circuit a lot') and in terms of his commercial conquests as well. He uses it to encourage confidences (thus taking advantage of its effects upon the behaviour of others), and then to press home his advantage in dominating them still further. It never seems to occur to him that he too may behave differently when he has been drinking and that, far from being in tighter control, he may just be tighter.

Harriet, his wife, although clearly somebody whose drinking is to an extent problematic, is very self-aware. She knows full well that drinking is so much part of her lifestyle that it has become completely integrated and is indistinguishable from other social activities. Drinking, for her, simply is.

What emerges from this discussion is the very wide range of purposes that drinking can have for different people. Nor will different purposes necessarily be compatible with each other, from a rational point of view. Deborah is the only person to complain that she sometimes experiences hangovers and even she admits they only influence her intended drinking behaviour very temporarily. That is why it is important to try to understand your own drinking style in a lot of detail. It is not enough to point to a few examples of alcohol-related health damage and expect that, by a single rational process, that will be enough to encourage moderate drinking practices. People do not operate with that comfortable degree of rationality. Possible further consequences of behaviour are a great deal less forceful than the hidden springs that influence the behaviour in the first place.

Choosing to have a drink/Drinking without choosing

The final alternative in this series of drinking-style variables has to do with the extent to which the act of having a drink involves a deliberate choice. Later in this book some space will be devoted to improving what are often called 'decision-making skills' so that, if you do decide to have a drink, it is a choice which is actively made, rather than something you have simply drifted into. At this stage, however, it is worth recognizing that this is a less straightforward issue than it might appear at first sight. Drinking without choosing seems such a preposterous idea that it needs to be examined carefully.

Various important influences on drinking have already been noted. Consider what might be the strongest influences on the five people whose cases have provided the background material for this section of the book. Decisions to have a drink, like many other decisions, are not always exactly and exclusively what they seem.

Habit, for example, exerts an enormous influence. When Bill has a few drinks with his friends before the match on a Saturday, is he *choosing* to do so, or is it simply a habit that now involves no real choice? 'Loyalty counts for something, doesn't it?' he asks, recognizing that his Saturday lunchtime drinking is part of a consistent pattern. Another powerful influence is social pressure. Deborah's fear of looking stupid in her friends' eyes if she doesn't drink is a perfect example. In Michael's case, his occupation actually demands that he drinks. In Harriet's case, drinking seems to be the only way she can give some shape to her life.

These are all examples of ways in which something has blunted the edge of the choice, making it less of a deliberate and conscious act and more of a response to other sorts of pressures. If you believe that you always make a deliberate choice when you have a drink, try not drinking for a couple of weeks. Notice the explanations, excuses and prevarications you have to offer to explain your behaviour to others. Maybe avoiding embarrassment is as important a factor in choosing to have a drink as seeking to achieve modest euphoria.

Drinking in Context

Looking back over all these alternatives, remember that they are not black-and-white choices. Most people will be somewhere between the two extremes and their position will vary from time to time. Remember, too, that it is not a question of right and wrong. This section of the book is about trying to achieve an understanding of your own drinking and/or somebody else's. Maybe understanding your own drinking will help you understand somebody else's. Maybe looking in detail at somebody else's drinking will give you some insights into your own. Because, as was indicated earlier, hardly anybody drinks in isolation. Each individual's drinking behaviour is influenced by the drinking behaviour of the important people who surround him or her. Similarly, although the focus of this book is on drinking, it is not an activity that is sealed off from the rest of your life. On the contrary, drinking is so mixed in with your job, your leisure time, your friends, your family, your fears and aspirations, your emotional state, your health, your love-life, your age, your income, your religion, your race and your moral sense, that to think about your drinking is to think about all these other things too.

This section of the book has been an attempt to persuade you not to take drinking for granted. To keep things in proportion you need to remind yourself that drinking is only one part of your whole way of life. Not the other way round.

2. ALCOHOL – THE EVERYDAY DRUG

Very few people really think of alcohol as a drug. Most people think of drugs either as medicinal substances prescribed by their doctor, or as illegal substances linked with international crime and with pathetic, down and out addicts. At first sight alcohol seems a long way from either of these stereotypes. It is, however, worth pausing, taking a step back and seeing how close, after all, alcohol may be to both those views of how drugs are used in society.

At the beginning of the previous section the undoubted pleasurable aspects of drinking were emphasized. Many of these pleasurable aspects are the direct result of the drug effects of alcohol. Relaxation, sociability, mild disinhibition and an enhanced sense of well-being – these are all specific effects of moderate alcohol consumption and they all have specific roots in the way that alcohol acts upon different parts of the brain. A pharmacologist could account for all these effects in terms of changes in the brain chemistry of the drinker. This is one of the main reasons why people drink – they enjoy the way alcohol changes their consciousness. A modest sense of euphoria is a highly desirable state. In choosing to drink in a particular way, people are often using alcohol as a drug, just as they might use aspirin to control a headache, but without really recognizing that they are dealing with the drug effects of the substance.

Just as there are similarities between alcohol and medically prescribed drugs, so there are similarities between alcohol and illegal drugs as well. In place of international crime rings there is the international beverage industry, increasingly dominated by transnational corporations. As drinking styles grow less parochial – the huge increase in wine-drinking in Britain over the last twenty years is a good example, so there is a need for a sophisticated system of international trade to supply the whole range of beverages which the consumer demands. The beverage industry, of course, both stimulates and satisfies consumer demand in a continuous process, often looking to trends in drinking styles, such as the switch from dark to light spirits, five or ten years into the future. The beverage industry is, of course, tightly controlled by national regulations and international trade agreements. It is also concerned with the quality and purity of the product in a way that is quite the opposite of the adulterating processes which mark international drug trafficking.

The final similarity between alcohol and other drugs, both prescribed and illegal, is that it can lead to addiction. The figure of the heroin addict is a familiar stereotype on television and in the newspapers. Society is becoming increasingly aware that some commonly used medicines, such as Valium, can also produce an addiction of frightening severity. Alcohol addiction is something which will be discussed at greater length later in this section, but it is worth remembering at this stage that the very fact that addiction is possible and that it does indeed occur with greater frequency than is often recognized, is another reminder that alcohol is a drug – probably the most popular drug in the world.

But these are not just interesting similarities between alcohol and other drugs. What these similarities mean is that alcohol has to be treated with the same kind of caution that is reserved for all other drugs. The more drinking is taken for granted, the less likely it is that the drug effects of alcohol will be recognized for what they are. Although these effects are generally beneficial when they result from moderate consumption levels, they can of course be much more serious, even devastating, when drinking gets out of hand.

The other drug which, like alcohol, has become for many people a part of everyday life is, of course, tobacco. More recently, however, as awareness of the health risks associated with smoking has spread, people have started to take smoking less for granted. It is interesting to notice how, in public places like restaurants, cinemas and theatres, it is becoming increasingly common for some sections at least to be designated as non-smoking areas. This has been true of trains, buses, and airplanes for a number of years, but airlines and national railway companies are reporting that they are now having to increase their non-smoking seat allocations. Whatever may be happening to total cigarette consumption (which could easily remain high even if fewer people were smoking, provided that those who did smoke were consuming more cigarettes), society now seems to want some sort of limits to be imposed upon smokers.

Drinking is different from smoking in at least two important ways. First of all, unless the drinker has so much alcohol that he becomes unpleasantly drunk, drinking does not tend to annoy other people in the way that smoking does. While we hear a lot about 'passive smoking', meaning the smoke inhaled even by non-smokers as a result of being in the company of smokers, we do not hear much about 'passive drinking', or at least not in the same sense. Secondly, there can be no doubt that any smoking causes harm. Drinking, by contrast, provided that it is at moderate levels, seems to be associated with increased rather than decreased life expectancy. Some insurance companies have noted that people who are light drinkers tend to live a little longer on average than people who are either heavy drinkers or abstainers. There is even a suggestion that low levels of drinking can have a positive beneficial effect in reducing the risks of some kinds of heart disease, although it should be pointed out that heavier drinking certainly increases such risks substantially. In other words, while there is really very little good that can be said for smoking, drinking may be harmless and possibly (at low levels) even beneficial. It is also worth mentioning that drinking, at least in Britain and most other northern countries, has been around for a great deal longer than smoking and is therefore better integrated into existing cultural traditions.

In terms of its actual drug effects, however, it is really not necessary for drinkers to understand the precise action of alcohol on each organ of the body. What is important is to have some general sense of the way alcohol can lead to damage and of the sites within the body where damage is most likely to occur. As with other drugs, it is probably helpful to separate the short-term and the long-term effects of alcohol, although the short-term effects (which have to do with getting drunk on a single occasion) can occur in people who are experiencing long-term effects as well. Alcohol addiction will be discussed separately, and this section of the book will end with a brief description of the early warning signs which might alert you to the possibility that you or somebody close to you is drinking more than is good for health and well-being.

Short-term Effects

Strictly speaking, alcohol is a depressant. This does not mean that it necessarily makes you feel depressed; the everyday experience of most drinkers would clearly seem to contradict that. It simply means that its action as a drug is to depress certain activities of the central nervous system. The paradox – that alcohol is called a depressant, but actually seems to stimulate the drinker – is only an apparent one, since the main area of the brain which alcohol depresses is the one which normally censors behaviour and imposes various inhibitions upon speech and action. Thus, the way in which drinking seems to loosen the tongue and generally remove people's inhibitions is perfectly consistent with its pharmacological properties.

The short-term or *acute* effects of alcohol are those which relate to a single drinking episode. When people are under the influence of a drug, they are described as being 'intoxicated' and that word has come to have a wide range of popular meanings. In terms of alcohol, it is often used to mean the same thing as 'drunk'. Indeed, the English expression 'drunken driver' translates into American as DWI, 'driving while intoxicated'.

In relation to driving, the law imposes a specific limit upon the degree of intoxication permitted. This is measured by the proportion of alcohol in the bloodstream, usually expressed in terms of milligrams of alcohol per hundred millilitres of blood. In the UK, the present level above which it is illegal to drive is 80 milligrams of alcohol per 100 millilitres of blood. Some countries have different limits – 40, 50, 100 or even 120 – while others have no limits at all. The so-called blood/alcohol concentration is simply a way of quantifying, for legal purposes, a particular level of intoxication. It does not necessarily measure in behavioural terms how drunk you are. Some people are obviously better able to hold their drink than others. Different countries have chosen different levels because of the view they take about the statistical likelihood of increased accident rates. There is no absolute cut-off point up to which you are sober and after which you are drunk. Intoxication is a gradient, which is more or less steep for different people and even for the same person at different times.

One of the difficulties about a system of legislation based upon blood/alcohol concentrations is that many people have only the vaguest idea about how that translates into ordinary drinking practices. This is further complicated because few people take all their alcohol in a single concentrated dose. Most people will have several drinks over a period of one, two or more hours. After alcohol has been swallowed, it passes to the stomach and intestine and is then absorbed quite rapidly into the bloodstream, which carries it throughout the body. One of the organs to which it is carried is the liver, which actually does the job of breaking down or metabolizing the alcohol, thus ridding the body of its short-term effects. It takes the liver about an hour to deal with each drink (a drink, remember, being a half-pint of beer, a glass of wine or a single measure of spirits). That is why the effects of a heavy drinking session can stay with you for a long time after you have stopped drinking. Somebody who has had six pints of beer in an evening could still be legally over the limit when driving to work the next day.

If you want to have an approximate measure of the blood/alcohol concentration you are likely to have reached after a specific number of drinks, then you can use the table on the opposite page as a rough guide.

A few words of caution, however, about that table. It is only a *rough guide*, because there are considerable differences between individuals and even within the same individual at different times. Factors such as how tired you are, when you last ate, your mood and your expectations of the particular drinking occasion will all influence the absorption rate and the way you feel, speak and act. The figures in the table are approximate blood/alcohol concentrations for a man of seventy kilos or eleven stone. If you are lighter than that or if you are a woman, you have to reckon on the likelihood that your blood/alcohol levels will be even higher than those shown in the table. Remember also that you really have to calculate from the time you *stop* drinking, not from the time you start, or you will produce a very inaccurate estimate. And, finally, do not forget that the number of drinks (on the left-hand side of the table) is based upon *half* pints of beer and *single* measures of spirits.

Number of Drinks	Blood/alcohol concentration (milligrams of alcohol per 100 millilitres of blood)		
	After 1 hour	After 2 hours	After 3 hours
1	20	0	0
2	40	10	0
3	60	30	20
4	80	60	40
5	100	80	60
6	120	100	90
7	140	120	110
8	160	150	130
9	180	170	150
10	210	190	170

What, then, actually happens to somebody who goes on drinking? Again, it is less important to understand the pharmacological processes than the behavioural changes. These changes may be much more evident to other people than to the drinker, since one of the effects of alcohol is to blunt your self-awareness. If you doubt the truth of this observation, then you can carry out a simple experiment for yourself. Deliberately refrain from drinking at all on an occasion when you know that those who are with you are going to be drinking quite heavily. Any occasion, such as an evening in the pub or a dinner party, will serve for this experiment. You will be surprised at how obvious and predictable the changes in your companions are – changes which you too would be showing if you had been drinking as much as them.

At first, after one or two drinks, most of the effects are subjective, but a careful observer will notice that people are adopting slightly more relaxed postures and are perhaps a little more talkative than usual. This talkativeness increases with the next drink or two and will often be accompanied by more vehement gestures and more frequent laughter. People will interrupt each other more in the course of ordinary conversation. At this level of intoxication, they are in fact more likely to be involved in accidents because their physical coordination, their speed of reaction and their powers of judgement are all beginning to be adversely affected. It is likely that their movements will be more exaggerated.

Another couple of drinks and their physical coordination will be significantly impaired. An objective observer, seeing them for the first time, would be very likely to decide that they were rather drunk and not merely somewhat extrovert. In some cases balance will be adversely affected at around this level and they may stagger, particularly if they stand up suddenly. They will certainly be unfit to drive.

Any further alcohol beyond this level of intoxication is often associated with the less pleasant aspects of drunken behaviour. Vomiting, aggressive or violent acts, sudden mood swings (often involving extremes of remorse and elation) can all be precursors to actual loss of consciousness, which can easily occur at around the level of 300 milligrams of alcohol per 100 millilitres of blood. Beyond that level, important bodily functions are increasingly affected. Alcohol, indeed, works as an anaesthetic. At a level of 500 milligrams, the heart and lungs would no longer be able to function and the drinker would die. It is, of course, very rare for anybody to reach such a high level of intoxication, but occasionally deaths are reported – often individuals who have attempted for a bet to drink a whole bottle of spirits without stopping.

Without doubt, the greatest short-term risk is the increased chance of being involved in an accident. Traffic accidents are the most obvious example, but accidents can also occur at home or at work. A large proportion of accidental fires are caused by the carelessness of somebody who has had too much to drink. The classic story of the drunk man falling asleep with a lit cigarette in his hand is in reality all too frequent an occurrence. Similarly, ordinary domestic obstacles, like staircases, loose rugs or electrical appliances can all become potential hazards for someone whose judgement, reaction time and coordination have been impaired. In the factory, with dangerous machinery and a tendency to ignore safety regulations, the risks are even greater.

The other main reason why drunk people arrive at accident and emergency units is because they have been involved in some kind of fight. Often, these are fights between protagonists who are equally drunk and who are, perhaps, anaesthetized by alcohol to the pain caused by the injuries they are inflicting upon each other. At other times, of course, in cases of domestic violence, for instance, an innocent and sober person can become the victim of somebody else's drunken rage. All too often patterns of domestic violence, including child abuse, seem to be associated with longer-term problems and are the result of somebody who goes on and on drinking too much. The persistently battered wife or child is a theme which will be taken up in the next section. Sometimes, however, a single drunken episode can bring a hidden resentment to the surface or make an everyday difficulty suddenly intolerable. Then a quick blow can easily replace the alternatives of silence, explanation or concern. As often as not, such hasty action may be regretted afterwards, but it is neither wholly accidental nor is it, unfortunately, without its consequences, both emotionally and in terms of simple physical damage.

A drunken person, weaving an unsteady path along the pavement, may also present himself as a perfect victim for a quick mugging. Much has been written about the association between alcohol and crime: the majority of murderers have been drinking heavily in the hours immediately before they commit their crime; but so, it seems, have the majority of their victims.

It has been argued that alcohol actually provokes crime, inflaming those who otherwise lead law-abiding lives. Some people argue that drunken criminals are simply more careless than sober ones and therefore more likely to make mistakes and be arrested. Certainly, people who have had too much to drink are frequently indiscreet and wake up the next day to regret things they have said or done the night before. This, on the other hand, may be something towards which society prefers to turn a blind eye, recognizing it as a kind of doubtful but necessary 'time out' for the therapeutic release of inhibitions.

Long-term Effects

Usually, if drinking has become a cause for concern it is because of a pattern of regular heavy drinking rather than a single drunken episode. This is not just because repeated bouts of heavy drinking are more likely to lead to the adverse short-term effects described above. There is also a whole catalogue of long-term effects which are the results of prolonged excessive consumption. These *chronic* effects of alcohol are physical, mental and social. They do not necessarily all occur in the case of every chronic drinker, but it would be rare for somebody who consistently drinks too much to avoid some degree of damage in these areas. Different conditions set in after different lengths of time for different people. Some people are more vulnerable than others to particular kinds of damage. Only one thing is certain: nobody who drinks too much has any reason to think of themselves as invulnerable. A great deal of damage may already have occurred before you are ever aware of it.

In terms of medical damage, it is often said that no system of the body is immune to the effects of alcohol. The liver is, of course, the organ which is most frequently mentioned in terms of diseases caused by alcohol. Liver cirrhosis and alcoholic hepatitis are both very serious conditions which, if untreated, will invariably lead to premature death. Although some people are clearly more vulnerable to liver disease than others, this remains one of the best indications of the extent of alcohol problems in any country or community. One fact which has emerged from recent research is that women tend to develop alcoholic liver disease more rapidly than men and also at somewhat lower levels of consumption.

Although very moderate drinking may actually offer some protection against death from coronary heart disease, chronic drinking leads to fatty infiltrations of the heart muscle and it seems that there is an increase in almost every kind of circulatory disease. Excessive drinking raises the blood pressure and therefore contributes to a higher risk of having a stroke.

The stomach is the place where the body first starts to deal with alcohol, and there are various digestive diseases: stomach ulcers in particular are very common among people who drink excessively. Further back up the digestive tract, cancers of the tongue, mouth, throat and oesophagus can also occur.

Other diseases associated with heavy drinking include pancreatitis, tuberculosis, kidney failure and anaemia. In men, it can lead to impaired sexual performance and even to impotence. In pregnant women, even comparatively low levels of drinking can have harmful effects upon the foetus. In both men and women, it can lead to a numbness and loss of sensation in the fingers and toes, a condition known as peripheral neuritis. Finally, there is also an obvious facial deterioration in many heavy drinkers, who develop the characteristic puffy eyes, bulbous nose and prematurely aged or unnaturally flushed skin. Although these last examples are often used as the comic characteristics of the stage or cartoon drunk, they are actually vivid signatures of the long-term physical damage which alcohol can produce in the human body.

There are also many psychiatric conditions which are associated with excessive drinking. Some of them – like Korsakoff's psychosis and Wernicke's encephalopathy – are comparatively rare, but others are much more common. Depression and anxiety are both caused and exaggerated by alcohol. An accumulation of vague, irrational fears of unknown origin is one example of this kind of disturbance. Other heavy drinkers experience hallucinations and some become morbidly jealous: men may start searching their wives' handbags obsessively for evidence of imagined infidelities.

More common still is interference with the function of memory, both in the short and the long term. At its most basic, as recent research has shown, alcohol can actually cause brain atrophy, even at comparatively low regular doses. Indeed, this brain damage is now thought by some researchers and clinicians to be a more accurate and more telling indicator of general alcoholic morbidity than liver disease.

The most dramatic example of all is probably suicide. It has been estimated that male alcoholics are eighty times more likely to commit suicide than normal men. People's mental condition will also affect their chances of being involved in accidents, a topic which was mentioned in the section on short-term effects. It is generally agreed that more than half the people admitted to accident and emergency units have been drinking heavily and, although some of these are intoxicated as the result of single uncharacteristic drinking occasions, many appear to be people who regularly drink too much and indeed injure themselves at home, at work or on the roads all too frequently.

While the physical and mental damage caused by excessive drinking has its greatest impact upon the drinker, the social damage is more likely to involve other people. It is personal relationships which seem to suffer the most. Marital problems often involve one or both partners drinking too much and this can, of course, lead to increased likelihood of divorce. Domestic violence, too, occurs as a result of a pattern of regular heavy drinking. Battered wives often talk about the repeated drunken bouts which were associated with their husbands' attacks upon them. Child neglect and child abuse are both more common where one or both parents drink heavily. It seems that the heavy drinker often feels some kind of grudge against the world and seeks an easy way to take that out on somebody. All too often, the person chosen is the most vulnerable and also the closest to the drinker. The sad spectacle of neglected or assaulted children, including young babies, is not, of course, invariably connected to a pattern of regular heavy drinking, but the two seem to go together with telling frequency, as recent figures have brought to light.

Looking back over the dismal catalogue of long-term effects which has taken up the last few pages, it is important to emphasize that these are indeed the effects of *excessive* drinking and not of drinking as such. If all drinking led to such distress, damage and mayhem, then the immediate abolition of such a pernicious drug would become the pressing concern of every reasonable person. However, as the opening sections of this book have stressed, moderate drinking generally leads to pleasure, not to pain, and your main concern should be to try to ensure that your drinking remains within the bounds where such damage is unlikely to occur.

There are, of course, no absolutely safe limits. But it is possible to obtain some kind of estimate of health risks associated with different drinking levels. Earlier in this book you will have learned how to count the average number of drinks you consume, both on a daily and a weekly basis. Using the diary chart which you filled in then, and remembering that for these purposes a drink is *half* a pint of beer or a glass of wine or a *single* measure of spirits, it is possible to show how your drinking level relates to the risks of physical damage, focusing mainly on the liver and brain damage described above.

What emerges is a kind of gradient of health risks. You should use this graph by looking for your weight on the left-hand upright and then reading across to the number of drinks you have on an average day, which is shown along the bottom line. The point where your weight crosses with the average amount you drink will give you some idea of whether you are at low risk, or increased risk of experiencing physical damage, or whether, indeed, it is likely that damage will already have occurred, even if you are not aware of it.

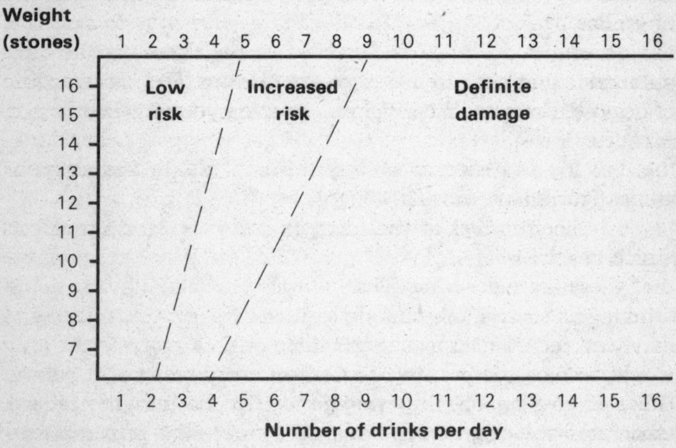

What this graph shows is the risk of *physical* damage. As you can see, there is no hard line between one category and the next. Obviously, the further you go into the 'Definite damage' area, the more serious the health problems are going to be.

Remember, too, that even in the 'Low risk' area, you are not necessarily safe to drive a car.

Graphs of this kind can only offer rough guidelines. This one is based upon average *daily* consumption levels. However, since it is drinking *habits* which are important as an indication of overall drinking style, it is necessary to look also at *weekly* consumption levels in order to find information to help you to assess the risks of alcohol-related damage. Later in this book the importance of setting and maintaining daily and weekly limits will be discussed in relation to strategies for avoiding problems. At this stage what is important is to have some sense of what these different levels of consumption mean in terms of the risks associated with them. The guidelines given here are based upon the results of research over the last ten years in Britain, France, Sweden, Canada and the USA.

Look back at your diary chart and focus now on the total of drinks for the *week*. As with the daily figure, it is necessary to consider a gradient of risks. There are no hard lines between the categories.

Up to 20 drinks per week: assuming that your drinking is not concentrated into one or two bouts, this level carries a low health risk. You should concentrate upon maintaining your drinking at this level.

21–30 drinks per week: at this level of drinking, the risks to your health are certainly increased. You should be thinking seriously about whether you want to continue drinking at this relatively risky level.

31–50 drinks per week: you are probably already doing yourself some harm, even if you are not aware of it yet. You should set about trying to bring your drinking down to a safer level.

Over 50 drinks per week: it is very rare for anybody drinking as much as this not to be harming themselves. Your physical and mental health will be deteriorating. All sorts of social problems may well be accumulating. You must take urgent steps to cut your drinking down drastically.

Much of the rest of this book will be devoted to how you can go about achieving a safer drinking style, including keeping to sensible consumption limits. This will be discussed firstly in relation to how you can control your own drinking, and secondly in relation to how you can help influence the drinking of somebody else. Since there is inevitably some overlap between the two sets of strategies, it is worth reading both sections.

Before turning to these 'how to' sections, you should consider briefly two topics which frequently cause concern: firstly, what exactly is meant by alcohol addiction or alcoholism; and secondly, whether there are specific early warning signs for which you should be on the alert.

Alcohol Dependence

When used in relation to alcohol, there is really no difference in meaning between the words 'addiction' and 'dependence'. People are dependent upon a substance when they are unable to give it up; they are addicted to a substance when they need to go on taking it in order to be able to function. The power of alcohol as an addictive drug has already been mentioned at the beginning of this section of the book. However, it is important to point out that dependence can manifest itself on a number of different levels. A distinction used to be drawn between psychological dependence (which was seen in terms of the *feeling* somebody had that they needed to go on taking the drug) and physical dependence (which was the requirement of the body for continued supply of the drug in order to stave off the physical withdrawal symptoms accompanying any period of abstinence). It is generally recognized now that there is no clear distinction to be drawn between psychological and physical dependence.

The other complicating factor is the concept of alcoholism. You will probably have noticed that the word has scarcely been used so far in this book. The concept of alcoholism as a distinct disease arose earlier this century and gathered force as a result of the combined efforts of the American medical profession and the influence of Alcoholics Anonymous. To the extent that it helped to remove guilt and social stigma from the individual sufferer it was clearly a considerable advance upon the previous concept of inebriety as a sin or moral flaw. What the disease concept of alcoholism also did, however, was to suggest that alcoholics were in some fundamental sense different from ordinary people. Using the analogy of allergic reactions and the way in which they operate, the suggestion was that alcoholics had some biochemical abnormality that meant they were predetermined to experience problems as a result of their drinking. This was sometimes defined in terms of genetic factors and sometimes in terms of personality factors. The implication was, however, that people who did *not* have this biochemical abnormality were not liable to become alcoholics.

While there does now seem to be evidence that some people have genetic predispositions which make them particularly likely to experience certain types of alcohol-related damage, such as liver cirrhosis, it has become clear that in general terms the amount people drink is the best predictor of whether or not they are likely to encounter alcohol-related damage of any sort at all. It does not seem, in other words, that there is a special group of people called 'alcoholics' who are in some fundamental sense different and who are bound to experience problems. Nor can it be said that the rest of the population is free from risk. Everybody who drinks too much is vulnerable.

Because this idea of genetic predisposition has become so inextricably entangled with the concept of alcoholism, and because of the confusion between psychological and physical dependence, an attempt was made in 1977 to resolve these difficulties by introducing a new term – a term which would not obscure the links between the causes of alcohol problems, the nature of alcohol addiction, and the medical and social consequences of excessive drinking. This new term – *the alcohol dependence syndrome* – has replaced alcoholism in the International Classification of Diseases and describes a more or less circular pattern. Once again, the relevance of the title of this book becomes apparent, for it does not matter where you begin upon the circle of the alcohol dependence syndrome, since it always brings you back to the point where you started. As drinking increasingly becomes the focus for an individual's life, so he will become increasingly accustomed to alcohol; as his tolerance to alcohol increases, so he needs to drink more and so his physical symptoms increase; in order to offset the physical symptoms, he feels the need to drink still more; this compulsion to drink more leads to drinking becoming increasingly the focus for his life. And so on: the same again.

Early Warning Signs

There have been various attempts to produce checklists of symptoms of drinking problems. They have often been inadequate: either they included symptoms that were so extreme that they were quite clearly signs of relatively severe drinking problems, or else they consisted of such vague and general signs that half the adult population might as a result fear themselves to be alcoholics. The concept behind this book is that a *complete drinking style* is important, not the appearance of one or two possibly unrelated symptoms. On the other hand, it is useful to have some kind of checklist, if only to confirm what you may already suspect.

In using this checklist of early warning signs, it is important again not to think of an absolute cut-off point between safe drinking and dangerous drinking. This is not one of those newspaper quizzes where, if you answer yes to only two or three questions, you can forget all about the problem. Clearly, the more of these signs which relate to your situation, the more serious the situation may be. There is, however, no reason to believe that the severity of the potential problems is related directly to the number of symptoms which you check on this list. Any cluster of symptoms is a cause for concern. But the absence of symptoms does not necessarily mean that your drinking is something which you can take for granted.

For convenience, these early warning signs are grouped under three general headings: social, psychological and physical.

Social signs:
Giving up other interests because of drinking.
Finding that you are drinking faster than your friends.
Missing meals in order to have a drink.
Being worried about how much you are spending on drink.
Needing a drink before you go to a party.
Ordering double quantities at closing time.
Choosing stronger drinks than a year or two ago.
Finding that other people criticize your drinking.

Psychological signs:
Feeling guilty about your drinking.
Finding that you cannot keep to a reasonable limit.
Being embarrassed at what you say and do when you have been drinking.
Being unable to sleep.
Experiencing sudden changes of mood.
Trying to convince yourself that your drinking is really all right.

Physical signs:
Frequent hangovers.
Inability to eat breakfast.
Difficulty in remembering events from the previous night.
Diarrhoea.
Bleary eyes.
Impaired sexual performance.
Frequent minor illnesses or accidents.

If you use this checklist it is important that you do so within the context of all that has already been said about drinking styles. Generally, in trying to assess whether or not a particular pattern of drinking should give you cause for concern, it is important to look for changes in style where these changes indicate that more drinking is taking place or that drinking is becoming increasingly central. For most people drinking is a pleasurable adjunct to social life; if it has become the centre of social life, so that the social life has just become an excuse to justify the drinking, then alcohol has become unhealthily important.

3. AVOIDING DRINKING PROBLEMS

Having looked at the pleasures and the pains of drinking and established some ground rules for describing drinking styles; having seen just how varied these pleasures, pains and styles can be, it is now time to turn to the question of how it is possible to *change* drinking styles in order to maximize the pleasure and minimize the pain. This section of the book will be concerned with what you can do as an individual to make the best of *your own* drinking. The next section will look at what you can do to help change *somebody else's* drinking. And the final section will provide information about how and where you can obtain further help, either for yourself or for somebody else.

Drinking, it is clear, is not a neutral activity. It is not something that just happens, without causes and without consequences. Having a drink, whether it involves ordering or pouring it yourself, or whether it involves accepting an offer from somebody else, means that you are making a choice. Your general drinking style, by extension, consists of a whole series of separate little choices, which can just as well be seen as a kind of general choice about the type of drinker you consider yourself to be. Nor are these choices separate from other choices you make about yourself. The kind of clothes you wear, the job you do, the places you spend your leisure time, all these choices and many more are linked to your drinking choices in a variety of different ways. Similarly, the drinking choices of the people who are close to you (family, friends, colleagues) will have an influence on your choices, just as your choices will influence them.

As you focus on change, try to be as clear as possible not just about what it is that is to be changed (your current drinking style) and what it is to be changed into (your ideal drinking style); you must also have a very clear sense of that process of making choices. In order to emphasize from the beginning how important it is that you should now take control – positive control, firm control, conscious control – of your drinking, this question of choice will be discussed in terms of decision-making skills.

Decision-making Skills

Making a decision is a conscious act. It should involve a firm and positive response to the situation which has created the need for it. Many decisions can be made quite quickly and without a great deal of effort. Some involve difficult and prolonged soul-searching. However, it is important to recognize that every decision has to do with resolving some sort of conflict.

To take a very simple example of a conflict to do with drinking which requires a decision to be made, you can imagine that a colleague at work has suggested that you join him for a drink after work in the pub down the road. In the fraction of a second which it takes you to accept or decline this invitation, it is likely that conflicting reasons will flick through your mind. They might look something like this:

Reasons to accept:	*Reasons to decline:*
It would be relaxing after a hard day's work.	I really ought to get home early tonight.
I'd like to spend some time with him outside work.	Maybe he's trying to get something out of me.
I'll probably be thirsty.	It's not really my favourite pub.
I like to seem friendly.	I like to seem independent.

All are relevant and influential reasons but, despite the conflict, are unlikely to prevent you making the decision. Most of the time you are probably scarcely even aware that such competing interests are involved in making simple decisions. As a first step, it may be helpful to try to be rather more aware than you would normally be of the reasons you find important in making decisions. Be sure that you do not just notice the reasons that justify the decisions you make; look also at the reasons you decide to ignore. You can look at this decision-making process in relation to your drinking behaviour and also in relation to any other aspect of your life, from simple questions ('Do you want to watch the Nine o'Clock

News?') to much more complicated ones ('Shall we visit your parents or mine for Christmas this year?').

Try jotting down lists like the one above, with reasons for and against. It may seem rather artificial at first but, if you are honest with yourself, you may already start learning something important about why you sometimes find yourself making wrong decisions. Perhaps you will find that you are terribly easily influenced by the opinion you think other people will have of you; or that you invariably tend to take the line of least resistance, even when you know you should choose the more difficult course. See if you can find a pattern to your decision-making, particularly in terms of those decisions which do not in the end work out so well for you.

The more drinking dominates your life and the more worried you are about whether it is leading you into difficulties, the stronger these conflicts are likely to be.

While the conflict used as an example above was a relatively minor one, and was probably relatively easily resolved, it could well have had unanticipated consequences. In accepting the offer of the drink, you could have taken the first step into a complicated emotional relationship with the other person; in arriving home later than expected, you could have tipped the balance in a precarious marital situation. In declining the offer, you could have found that you had missed the chance to collaborate on some important project which your colleague had wanted to discuss informally with you.

Such consequences remain, of course, impossible to predict. What is certain is that some conflicts are, by their very nature, more important and more problematic than others. Take as an example this time the conflict which arises when you decide, as you may well be doing if you are reading this book, that you want to cut down your drinking to a lower level.

Reasons to cut down:	*Reasons to continue:*
It's doing my health no good.	My best friends all drink as much as I do.
It's costing me a lot of money.	It gives me a lot of pleasure.

The family is suffering.	It helps me forget my worries.
I seem to be losing control of my own life.	You only live once.

For a complex decision like this, the lists could probably be extended considerably. It is important to notice two things about these lists. First of all, these are (in contrast to the first example) reasons to do with whole areas of your life and it is certain that they will have important consequences. These consequences *can* be anticipated. Secondly, there are legitimate reasons on both sides of the conflict. It will be even more difficult for you to change your drinking if you are not prepared to admit that there are also good reasons for you not to do so. Recognizing the legitimacy of those reasons and being prepared to confront them honestly with equally legitimate reasons for deciding against them, is an important step in the process of feeling that you are committed to making changes at all.

Keeping a Drinking Diary

Having decided that you do want to change your drinking behaviour, one of the changes you will probably want to make – perhaps the most basic change of all – is in the area of quantity and frequency. Earlier in this book (page 18) you learned how to achieve a reasonably accurate measure of the quantity of alcohol consumed, and on page 21 you filled up a diary for your last week's drinking. It is now time to use those same techniques for the purpose of monitoring your drinking.

In its simplest form, a drinking diary is a factual record of how much you have actually had to drink each day. If all you are seeking is to achieve a modest reduction in your current drinking level, then a diary chart like the one on page 21 may well prove sufficient. You should copy it out on to a file card or something of that sort – something that you can carry around with you in your wallet or handbag. Then, at the end of each drinking occasion (and remember, it is possible that a day may contain more than one drinking occasion – it could be lunchtime, after work and later in the evening) just jot down the total number of standard drinks that you have consumed. It can be done very easily and inconspicuously. If you wait until later, you may forget or estimate inaccurately. At the end of the day, work out your total for that day. And, at the end of the week, add up your daily totals to give you your weekly total.

On pages 59 to 60 of the section on long-term effects, the sorts of limits you should be thinking about for safer drinking were suggested, in terms of both daily and weekly consumption. These can be used as guidelines for interpreting your diary and for checking how successful you are being in keeping out of the more dangerous areas of heavier drinking.

Many people find that the very act of keeping a diary is itself a helpful control over their drinking, since it makes them more conscious of the choices they have made and of the way these choices build up into a pattern. In this sense, particularly if your drinking is not very heavy, but is just a little more than you would ideally like, the simple drinking diary can act as a kind of watchdog for you. If this is to be an effective process, then it is important that you take the trouble to maintain the diary over a reasonable period of time, probably a few months, in order to account for seasonal variations in your drinking. It is also essential that you do not just choose to let your diary lapse on those occasions when you decide, for whatever reason, to drink more heavily than usual. The value of the diary depends absolutely on the extent to which it is an accurate reflection of your drinking.

Setting Yourself Limits

For most people who are actively trying to change their drinking behaviour, the simple form of diary described above may prove inadequate. What it does is simply to record after the event how much was actually drunk on that occasion. Many people who are trying to change find it necessary to plan how much they think they *ought* to drink on each occasion as well as recording how much they actually *do* drink. This involves making even more conscious the sense of a running total of drinks as the means to monitor quantity and frequency.

There are various ways of achieving this. The first is to produce a modified version of the drinking diary, which also includes a column for your goal – that is to say, for the total maximum number of drinks which you wish to allow yourself. If you tend to have only one drinking occasion each day, then the diary chart can be modified simply by adding that extra column to the existing form:

	Beer	Spirits	Wine	Sherry, etc.	TOTAL	GOAL
Monday						
Tuesday						

If, however, it is quite common for you to drink on more than one occasion each day, then you may find it easier either to split each day into two:

		Beer	Spirits	Wine	Sherry, etc.	TOTAL	GOAL
M	Lunchtime						
	Evening						
T	Lunchtime						
	Evening						

or else, if your drinking is very irregular, to make up a fresh card for each day, collecting them together at the end of the week:

	Beer	Spirits	Wine	Sherry, etc.	TOTAL	GOAL
Morning						
Lunchtime						
Afternoon						
Dinnertime						
Evening						
WHOLE DAY						

As you become more accustomed to counting your drinks and as the equivalent strengths of the different beverages require less effort to remember, you will probably be able to stop having to list all the different beverage types separately. Most people, in any case, tend not to mix their drinks on any single drinking occasion, even though they may drink a wide range of different beverages in the course of an average week. Once you are accustomed to the process, to the equivalents and to your own drinking pattern, you may be able to devise a simplified version of this card, which could look something like this:

		TOTAL	GOAL		TOTAL	GOAL		TOTAL	GOAL
Monday	Lunchtime			Evening			Whole Day		
Tuesday	Lunchtime			Evening			Whole day		

Whichever form of diary chart best suits your lifestyle, the important point is that the GOAL column should be filled in *before* the drinking occasion, preferably at the start of each day or, even better, at the start of each week. In setting yourself goals for how much you think you ought to drink, you should bear in mind not only the safer drinking limits on pages 59 and 60, but also what you think you can realistically achieve. If you set yourself goals that are unrealistically strict, then you are likely to become discouraged very quickly indeed when you find that you really cannot keep to them. On the other hand, there is little point in setting yourself limits which are so high into the area of risky drinking that all you are doing is making the most marginal difference to the quantity that you consume. What you need to achieve is a balance between the recommended limits and your own personal capacity.

There is no reason to think of the limits which you set yourself as being fixed for all time. You may, for example, want to reduce your drinking gradually over a period of several weeks, cutting it down a little more each week, rather than making one single drastic reduction. There is no hard and fast rule here. Some people cope better with a gradual reduction, others with a firm cut-off point. In general, the most difficult strategy to operate is the one which appears the easiest – namely, gradually cutting down over a period of weeks. This is because your willpower to stick to your planned limit may be weaker after you have had a few drinks than it was before you started drinking. The temptation to have just one more can be very strong if you have had less to drink than you were accustomed to but enough to weaken your resolve.

On the other hand, if you can make that system work, it is clearly the smoothest in that it causes little disruption to your lifestyle. It may depend upon the extent of the change you are introducing. Some people even find it helpful to abstain from alcohol completely for a week or two and then start drinking again at their low limit. The only thing to do is to try the technique which you think will suit you best and, if that fails, to try the others.

Although you may be setting yourself quite strict daily or weekly limits, you should not necessarily be so rigid that you are not prepared to give yourself a day off if the occasion really does warrant it. It is essential that you use this relaxation of limits for really special occasions and not for every Saturday night, but there are times when normal, unproblematic drinkers do have a bit more to drink than they normally do. If such an occasion is coming up, then look carefully at how much more than usual you want to allow yourself. If you have already thought about it and made a rational decision, you are a great deal more likely to keep to it than if you have pretended to yourself that the occasion presented no difficulties, in which case, without a limit in mind, you might find yourself slipping back into very heavy drinking.

Just as with the simpler form of diary chart, it is important to keep a note of how much you are drinking *at the time* and not the next day. Then you can do something about it. You can slow down or stop your rate of consumption.

Some people find it difficult or embarrassing to keep a diary chart because they do not want their friends to know that they are trying to cut down their drinking. Often, such a fear is ill-grounded, since friends may prove very supportive of your efforts. However, if you have good grounds for believing that friends might indeed mock you or undermine your efforts, there are other strategies you can use. Firstly, you can explain that you are trying to slim and that you need to count your drinks because you are watching your calories. People who might feel threatened by your efforts to cut down (that is probably why they mock) are less likely to take a hostile attitude to something as 'respectable' as slimming. Alternatively, you can suggest that there are medical reasons for you to cut down your drinking (which is true enough – remember the section on long-term effects). Most people respect the advice of doctors and there is no reason for them to know that the advice came at second hand.

It may be that you feel neither of these strategies would prove effective, but that you still want to have some kind of physical record of how much you have consumed on any drinking occasion. Even if you do fill in your diary chart at the end of a drinking occasion, you may feel you want a surer method of keeping a running total. What you need is some inconspicuous method of counting the number of standard drinks you have consumed. It is relatively easy to devise a system which will work for you. If, for example, you had set yourself a limit of four drinks (remember, that is only two pints of beer), then you could put four coins into one pocket of your jacket. As you had each drink, you could transfer one coin to a different pocket. Or you could make marks with a pencil or even with your thumbnail on the edge of a beermat. Or you could tear a scrap of paper into pieces, one tear for each drink. There are plenty of methods which you could use, which nobody would ever notice. Then you could transfer the total to your diary chart at the first convenient opportunity.

Sometimes, of course, drinking occasions arise which you had not planned. Somebody unexpectedly invites you round to the pub. Somebody drops by with a bottle of wine. When that happens, all you need to do is simply to set yourself in your head a limit for how much you want to drink on that occasion. You will be accustomed to doing it already for planned drinking occasions and the principles you will need to use will be just the same. There is no need to feel flustered or unsettled by such occasions. They will, of course, have an impact upon your daily total, but you can then take that into account in setting your goals for the rest of the week.

Pacing Yourself

Time can often seem elastic to you when you are drinking and socializing. Sometimes, minutes seem to drag by with slow and ponderous regularity; at other times, an hour can have passed almost as soon as it has begun. These impressions are influenced by how much you are enjoying yourself and can also be exaggerated by the drug effects of alcohol. It is in just such circumstances that it can prove particularly difficult to keep to the self-imposed limits which you have set for that drinking occasion, if only because you find that you have reached your limit far more quickly than you had expected. You are therefore faced with a dilemma: either you abandon the pleasure of staying on in an enjoyable situation; or you knowingly exceed the number of drinks which you had set as your limit for that occasion.

The best way to avoid that difficulty is to pace your drinking as regularly as possible. Most bars have clocks which are clearly visible. If you have set yourself a limit of four drinks and you expect to stay in the bar for something like an hour and a half, then you can allow yourself half a pint of beer every twenty minutes. The same principle can be made to apply if, for example, you have been invited out to dinner. Indeed, it can be even easier in those circumstances, since many people now choose to dilute their wine with mineral water. You can use that technique to ensure that, without appearing to disdain someone's hospitality, you are nevertheless always within the limits which you have set yourself for the evening.

It may take some practice before you are able to pace your drinking in a natural way. Psychologists have noticed that people who drink very heavily tend to gulp their drinks rather than sipping them. One important part of learning to pace your drinking may involve deliberately drinking rather more slowly. Lift the glass to your lips less frequently and take smaller swallows of the beverage. Let go of the glass between sips rather than holding on to it all the time. Whatever you do, do not speed up your rate of consumption to match the drinking rate of other people. If everybody did that, they would all soon end up drinking like alcoholics.

An extension of the trick with the watered wine is to alternate between alcoholic drinks and soft drinks. It is quite possible to do this without anybody noticing. A straight ginger ale looks just the same as a whisky and ginger; the same is true for a gin and tonic or a vodka and tomato juice. Beer drinkers can try ordering half pints instead of pints or drinking shandy instead of bitter. Special strength lagers and extra-large measures (such as schooners of sherry) should be avoided.

The influence of some drinking situations (such as a group of friends who meet regularly at a particular pub) may be especially strong. It is even possible that the influence will be so strong that you are forced to choose to give up going there with them. Before it reaches that point, however, you can try other self-limiting techniques, which may be sufficient to ensure that you do not drink more than you really want to. You can try arriving a little later than usual or you can bring with you only just enough money to pay for the number of drinks you have set yourself as a limit. While neither of these techniques guarantees absolute success, they may be sufficient to strengthen your resolve in a difficult situation and to make it just that bit easier for you to stay within your limits.

Finally, if you can feel that you are likely to exceed your limits on a particular occasion, create a deliberate delay for yourself. Excuse yourself for five minutes. Go outside or to the lavatory. Tell yourself firmly that you are in control of your own life. Remind yourself of the reasons why you chose the limit that you set yourself. Ask yourself if you really do want to have that extra drink. Sometimes you may decide that you do. Much more frequently, the delay will give you the breathing space necessary to decide that you prefer, after all, to stick to your original plan.

Rewards and Punishment

The whole point of setting yourself limits is to ensure that they mean something to you and that you believe in them. If you are cynical about their validity or, worse still, if you consciously cheat yourself by drinking more than your limit and failing to record your over-consumption, then the exercise is clearly futile. That is why you need to think carefully about your limits, reassessing them periodically, and that is why you need to feel good about yourself when you keep to your limits and bad about yourself when you exceed them.

To some extent, the fact of having set the limits and – more important – the fact of writing them down and keeping a record of your successes and failures, will act as a reward in itself. A week in which you have consistently kept to your limits will seem like receiving a good report card from school at the end of term. If there is somebody else who knows about your attempt to cut down your drinking, then you should show them your weekly drinking diary on a regular basis. As they share your pleasure in your successes and your disappointment in your failures, so their feelings will reinforce your own.

However, you may want to set up another, more distinct system of rewards and punishments. There is no doubt that we are all more likely to repeat actions for which we are rewarded and to avoid those for which we are punished. Usually such rewards and punishments are arranged by an outside agency (your boss, your parents, the law of the land), but there is no reason why you should not arrange them for yourself. If you do so, you obviously have to make sure that you keep to these arrangements. It may help to write them down, or to confide them to a friend or member of your family. Make sure that you really do review your progress, or lack of it, regularly and that you carry out the system properly.

The sorts of rewards which you might give yourself for having kept within your limits during a particular week should probably be those little luxuries which you would not normally allow yourself. Things like a visit to the cinema, buying some new clothes, or even an extra hour in bed on Sunday morning. They should not be impossibly grandiose, but neither should they be so trivial that they scarcely seem like rewards at all.

Similarly, if you are punishing yourself for having failed to keep to your limits, then the punishment should cause you some inconvenience, but should not be so severe that it causes you pain disproportionate to the offence. One scheme which some people find very persuasive is to have a private arrangement that for each extra drink they have consumed in a week they will give a set sum of money (say £1) to their *least* favourite cause. There is, after all, nothing that a staunch Labour Party supporter would less like to do than to contribute a fiver to the Tories. It is not just the loss of the money that is the punishment, but also the knowledge that it is being used to work against what you believe in. Contributing the money to your favourite charity, although a possible strategy, is less effective.

You can use money as the basis of a longer-term reward system as well. If you estimate how much you would have spent on drinking if you had kept to your original level of consumption and then subtract the amount you have actually spent, you can put the difference into a special savings account which you use, after a period of a few months, to give yourself a more substantial reward, such as a holiday that you would not otherwise have been able to afford.

Buying Rounds

This is one situation which can undermine all your carefully laid plans: you find yourself with a group of friends, all of whom are taking it in turns to buy drinks for everybody. The practice of buying rounds can have three adverse consequences: it might mean that you have to consume as many drinks as there are individuals in the group; it might mean that there will be a tendency for everybody to pace their drinking on the fastest drinker in the group, so as not to leave him with an empty glass; and it might mean that you feel a strong social pressure not to order soft drinks.

By far the best method of dealing with rounds is to avoid letting yourself be trapped into them in the first place. *'No thanks,'* you can say, *'I'm not going to be able to stay long, so I think I'll just buy my own.'* You may be surprised to find that other members of the group will welcome such a suggestion and will also offer to buy their own drinks. Many people resent the tyranny over their drinking styles which round-buying imposes. There have even been attempts to ban round-buying by law. From a public health point of view it is generally seen as a factor which leads to higher overall consumption. It is forbidden to depict the buying of large rounds of drinks in alcohol advertising.

If, despite your efforts, your first drink is bought for you by whatever loud-mouthed individual has pushed himself forward as leader of the group, then two alternatives remain open for you. You can either make sure that it is you who buys the second or third round. As you stand up to go to the bar, you can say: *'I've really got to be going after this, so do let me buy this round.'* This is, of course, an expensive strategy and one which means you may have to cut short your evening with your friends, but at least it provides an elegant exit from a long tunnel of continuing drinking.

Once you have become accustomed to pacing yourself and feel confident in your ability to make a single drink last as long as you want it to, the simplest method of all for dealing with rounds becomes possible. Accept an initial pint of beer from whoever buys the first round and then drink it very, very slowly indeed. That way, when it comes time for the second round to be bought, you will probably be only a little way into your pint. It will look like a virtually full glass. Thus, when you are asked what you would like, you can very easily reply, *'Oh, I've still got one. I'm fine this time, thanks.'* Since buying rounds is rather an expensive way of drinking and since anyone who does not need a drink is one less to buy, few people will question your assertion. With practice, you can easily nurse a pint or two of beer throughout a whole evening's drinking.

The other alternative is to insist upon having soft drinks, either all the time or at least every other drink, depending upon the size of the round. This is not as difficult to do as it may seem before you have tried it. The next two sections look at techniques for refusing drinks and at non-alcoholic alternatives.

Refusing Drinks

Many people find the actual act of refusing a drink very difficult. They become confused and embarrassed, handle the situation badly and end up feeling obliged to consume a drink which they did not really want in the first place. Sometimes these difficulties can be even greater if it is clear in advance that a drink is going to be offered. Then the anticipation of the embarrassment seems to double its intensity.

This is quite different from simply experiencing an urge to have a drink. You may well feel such an urge from time to time while you are trying to cut down your drinking. As often as not, it will be an urge to have *another* drink, rather than an urge to have the first drink. You will soon learn how to refuse yourself. Some of the techniques described above in the sections about setting limits and pacing yourself (pages 69 to 76) will help you cope with this. Urges are very seldom truly irresistible. When people say they are, it usually means that, in terms of decision-making, they decided the reasons to drink were stronger for them at that particular time than the reasons not to do so. Learning to control these urges has a lot to do with taking a more rational approach to decision-making.

The same sort of approach is called for when learning to turn down offers of drinks from other people. The reason that a refusal may cause you embarrassment has less to do with drinking as such than it has with the social meaning which drinking has acquired. By refusing a drink, it may seem as if you are telling the person who has offered it that you dislike them; as if what you are really doing is rejecting them. Especially since an offer of a drink is frequently a sign of hospitality, friendship or personal interest, a refusal may be interpreted as a rejection of the sympathy that was being extended. So the first step in learning how to refuse a drink is to realize that it need not mean that you are rejecting the person who is offering it to you.

As soon as you realize that yourself, you can be more rational about coping with the refusal, just as you have learned to be more rational about coping with your own urges to drink. You can express your refusal in terms which make it clear that it is, indeed, only the drink itself which you are turning down, and not what the drink might symbolize.

There are various forms of words you can use. Some rely upon 'excuses' from beyond the drinking occasion – things like:

'I'm afraid I mustn't. Doctor's orders.'

'Listen, I'm trying to lose weight. Don't tempt me. Just a slim-line tonic, please.'

'No, I'm driving, so I'd rather not. Just a coke would be fine.'

What is important about these ways of refusing a drink is that they rely for their effectiveness upon bringing into play a set of values (doctor's orders; slimming; driving) with which most people are likely to feel in sympathy. They are, if you like, 'respect-able excuses' which are probably going to be accepted at face value without much comment or adverse criticism.

As you become more experienced at turning down drinks, you may find that you need to rely upon excuses less and less. You may find it a lot easier and less embarrassing than you had expected to be straightforward about your disinclination to drink alcohol:

'No, no more thanks. Really.'

'No thanks. I'm not drinking.'

'That's kind of you, but no.'

Whichever approach you adopt, the same general principles apply. The first is that you should say your piece briefly and firmly. If you waffle, hesitate, backtrack or try to offer elaborate explanations, people will soon sense that there is something behind your refusal. Either because they are curious to find out what that might be or because they sense a lack of resolve in you, they are very likely to argue with you and to contradict your reasons. The further you get drawn into an argument about your reasons for turning down the drink, the more likely it is that you are going to end up either accepting the drink after all (the line of least resistance) or creating a socially unpleasant incident (by sticking to your resolve).

Although you need to be firm in your statement, it is just as important that you should be polite. Being assertive is a different thing from being aggressive. Remember that it is just the drink that you are turning down. Too vehement a refusal is just as likely to provoke an awkward response as one which is too hesitant. Children are forever being told to remember to say 'please' and 'thank you'. This is sound advice for adults as well. If your refusal is courteous and polite, it is much more likely to be accepted at face value.

There are, of course, some people who never seem able to take no for an answer. That can be because they really are using the offer of a drink to make a big symbolic gesture towards you, telling you without explicit words that they like you and want you to like them too. Or it can be because they are just boorish and unpleasant people without civilized social skills. In either case, you have to be prepared to repeat yourself if they press you, maybe varying the words slightly, but not the reason. If you repeat your refusal two or three times, most people will accept that you mean what you say. In a situation where you are being pressed repeatedly to have a drink it is very important to remember to remain polite. Even if there is embarrassment, you can at least derive some satisfaction from the fact that your behaviour did not cause it.

Since refusing drinks is something which causes people difficulty and since it is pretty central to the whole process of controlling your drinking behaviour, it may actually be worth practising the techniques in private before trying them out in public. Decide which approach you find most comfortable and then try it out, either in front of a mirror or with a close friend who knows what you are trying to achieve. Like anything else, it is just a question of getting used to saying the words without feeling that they are somehow unnatural or artificial.

A final danger in refusing drinks lies in being more explicit than you need to be. Sometimes, once you have established a formula with which you feel comfortable, you automatically trot your explanation out every time you are asked. As others grow accustomed to the fact that you drink a bit less than you used to, they will just accept it without particular emphasis. All you may need to do is to lay your hand across the top of your glass, shake your head and smile. But do remember the smile, for without that the best-intentioned refusal can seem cold and churlish.

Alternative Drinks

This is really just to expand a little upon the basic point which has already been made – namely, that a drink need not necessarily mean an alcoholic drink. It may be a great deal easier to accept an orange juice or a coke instead of a pint or a martini than to turn down the offer of a drink completely. It is, however, worth practising how you request a non-alcoholic drink so that it does not sound lame or awkward. There is certainly no reason why accepting a tomato juice should have any less symbolic meaning than accepting a vodka and tomato juice. Unless it is the intention of the person making the offer to get you drunk (in which case, whatever happens, you are a great deal better off remaining sober), then the choice of beverage is something which is simply to do with what you like drinking, since who you like drinking with remains the same in either case.

If you usually drink beer or wine, then there are a number of non-alcoholic beers (especially lagers) and wines on the market now which taste very much like their alcoholic equivalents but which are either completely or substantially alcohol-free. It may be worth your while experimenting with the different brands available in order to find out which you prefer. If you regularly drink in the same pub or restaurant, the manager will soon recognize that it is worth his while stocking your favourite brand in order to keep your custom.

While there is no non-alcoholic equivalent to spirits, two

important points should be made. Firstly, as has already been noted, a ginger ale is, as far as other people are concerned, indistinguishable from a whisky and ginger ale, and a tonic water indistinguishable from a gin and tonic. People, such as diplomats and even members of the Royal Family, who have to attend frequent functions at which they are expected to drink, have long ago learned to ask whoever is in charge of the bar to make sure that they receive only the mixer and not the spirit. Secondly, as cocktails are once again becoming popular, the opportunities to create splendid non-alcoholic cocktails, complete with all the trimmings of ice, tiny paper parasols and bits of fruit and vegetables, are really quite considerable. The character of a cocktail lies as much in what it looks like as in what is actually in it. You will find that most books of cocktails contain quite a wide range of non-alcoholic versions, and there is no reason why you should not invent some of your own.

In fact the present social trend seems to be favouring those who do not always want to drink alcohol. Increasingly, pubs are offering coffee as a regular beverage available during opening hours, and indeed sometimes outside opening hours as well. Even tea, still Britain's most popular beverage, is beginning to appear in some pubs. And the manufacturers of soft drinks are recognizing that, just because a drink is soft, it does not need to be boring. A wider range of non-alcoholic drinks which are to be consumed for their own sake rather than as mixers will be appearing on the market during the coming years. You can help to speed that process up by contributing to the demand for them. Nor need you feel that you are letting your local landlord down by ordering soft drinks, since they actually give him a higher profit margin than most alcoholic beverages.

Finally, in choosing to drink non-alcoholic beverages sometimes you are contributing to another social trend – the growing recognition that, despite its many virtues, alcohol is not always the sophisticated, civilized and sexy commodity that is displayed in the advertisements. People, it seems, are finally coming to realize that it is smarter not to get smashed.

Changing Your Drinking Style

The long section earlier in this book which was devoted to understanding drinking styles looked at a whole range of different variables. In reading that section, you will have already begun to gain a sense of which sorts of drinking styles are likely to be associated with lower levels of risk. The question now is how you can use that understanding to help you to avoid drinking problems.

The time that you have your first drink of the day is one important factor over which you can exercise considerable control. It has already been pointed out that people who feel they need a drink as soon as they wake up or shortly afterwards are probably seriously alcohol-dependent, and are really in the same position as the heroin addict who starts to crave the drug as soon as the effects of the previous fix begin to wear off. If your addiction is so serious that you feel you need to drink early in the day, then you may well find it difficult to change your drinking style without some sort of outside help. There is no reason why you should not have a go yourself, but you should also be aware of the range of professional and voluntary services that exist to help you if you are not successful. These services are listed in the final section of this book, from pages 123 to 127.

If you are trying to change your drinking style so that you end up consuming less alcohol, then lunchtime drinking is one area which is worthy of special attention. Even in terms of maintaining reasonable efficiency at work in the afternoon, two standard drinks (a pint of beer or its equivalent) is probably the upper limit for most people. If your intention is to make a real dent in your regular drinking and if you always tend to have a few drinks at lunchtime, then it is obviously an occasion for using all those skills in limitation, pacing and refusal that have been described earlier in this section. Maybe you should even consider cutting out alcohol altogether from your lunchtime habits. This means that you have to change the place where you usually eat lunch or choose to eat with a different group of people. If your lunchtime location and your companions were leading you into heavier alcohol consumption than you really wanted, then a change may be quite sensible from the point of view of your continuing good health.

If you decide that you really do like to have a drink at lunchtime and that giving it up would cause more difficulties than you feel are justified, then you should make sure that you also have sufficient food. There is nothing more likely to exaggerate the acute effects of alcohol than an exclusively liquid lunch. While beer does contain some important vitamins – and all alcoholic drinks contain their fair share (some more than their fair share) of calories, the alcohol will be absorbed particularly rapidly into the bloodstream if there is no food in the stomach to slow up that process. Any sense of feeling revived by a couple of quick drinks at lunchtime with nothing to eat is purely illusory and very short-lived.

At the other end of the scale, if you are frequently involved in lavish business lunches you need to be especially careful. Drinks before, during and sometimes also after the meal can add up to a heady total. Practise the techniques described above for limiting your consumption. Let your glass of wine stand virtually untouched save for the occasional sip, while actually slaking your thirst with mineral water: you will retain the impression that you are participating in the drinking ritual, but you will have drunk only a single glass of wine by the end of the meal. You may be surprised to find that the relative clear-headedness associated with a lower consumption level actually enables you to excel at business transactions which were previously shrouded in a vague alcoholic haze. Increasing consciousness of fitness and health is also tending to make business lunches rather less attractive than they used to be. Middle-aged men, worried about ulcers and heart failure, are already recognizing the dangers of regular heavy midday meals. Heavy drinking is just one further unhealthy burden to bear. Be prepared to say as much if others try to press you into eating and drinking more than you actually want.

If you cannot avoid the occasional lunch accompanied by a lot of drinking, then it is certainly a good idea not to drink any more on that particular day. This is something which you should be especially aware of, since many people find that, if they have had more to drink than usual at lunchtime, they are more rather than less likely to feel like a drink in the evening as well.

Good habits (in the context of this book, those habits which are associated with lower levels of alcohol consumption) can sometimes drift into more doubtful areas. For example, if you usually have a drink with a colleague at the end of the working day, you should make sure that your single drink does not become two or three or that you do not start leaving work five, ten and then fifteen minutes early in order to get to the pub. Similarly, anybody who slips away from work for a quick drink when the pubs open, either in the morning or in the afternoon, is probably relying upon alcohol to a much greater extent than he realizes. People who work at home, such as housewives, and whose work is probably more monotonous than they would like, may be especially prone to let a simple habit, such as having a small glass of sherry with their solitary lunch, drift into a problem without really noticing that it is happening.

Generally, evening drinking is not something you will want to curtail too much. It may be that one way of drinking a little less is simply to arrive at the pub later or leave earlier. But since evening drinking is often a more relaxed occasion than drinking at other times of the day, you may need to remind yourself more frequently about the decision you have taken to change your drinking style. If you go to the pub every single night, then a good strategy may be to cut down the number of drinking occasions. A later section will consider what alternative activities you can take up to fill time previously spent in drinking (see page 96).

The earlier in the day you think about having your first drink, the more likely it is that alcohol is playing too important a part in your life. If drink is the first thing you think about when you wake up, then you are almost certainly already in difficulties. If, on the other hand, you never think about drinking unless somebody else suggests it, then you are very unlikely to have a problem. Most people are somewhere in between these two extremes. You can use this question to test yourself from time to time, just to see if drinking is becoming more or less important to you. The more drinking dominates you, the more likely it is that you need to dominate your drinking.

As you take control of *when* you drink in order to influence *how much* you drink, so you will see how you need to take control of *where* you drink and *whom* you drink *with* as well. It has already been suggested that one way to help cut out lunchtime drinking would be to go somewhere different with a different group of friends. Looking back at the section on drinking styles on pages 36 to 40, you will see that there was some discussion of how different drinking environments imposed greater or lesser controls upon the drinker. A landlord in a pub, for example, will be happy for his customers to spend as much as possible in his establishment, provided that they do not get drunk and cause trouble. Thus, one set of influences (the furnishings, the lighting, the music, the salted peanuts and crisps) will be intended to increase your consumption. At the same time some of the same influences (the furnishings, lighting and music) will be designed to make you feel relaxed, a mood which will be reinforced by the verbal or physical control which the landlord exerts over rowdy customers. Drinking environments with stricter controls over behaviour, whether these controls are explicit (rules of the house) or implicit (nobody would think of doing that here) are more likely to prove an effective limiting factor over excessive consumption. The more relaxed the environment, the fewer limits are likely to emerge.

There is, of course, something of a conflict here. Most people like to feel relaxed when they are drinking. The pub is still the favourite place to spend leisure time outside the home. The optimum situation is that where the rules are so much in keeping with what the drinkers want to do in any case that they only become evident as rules when somebody steps out of line. If you are looking for ways to reinforce your decision to cut down your drinking, then you may in any case need to think about changing the place you regularly drink. It is important in these circumstances that you choose somewhere which has rather stricter drinking norms (i.e. unwritten rules), rather than somewhere which allows or even encourages drunkenness.

A good example of how this principle operates can be seen in the reduction in violence at football matches since alcohol was banned from the grounds. It is not a simple matter of saying that alcohol makes people violent. Rather, in an environment where there is already a lot of rivalry and heated emotions, and where the unwritten rules of the crowd condone a certain level of aggressive behaviour, alcohol has the effect of gearing up the aggression which, in turn, gears up the drinking still further. By taking the alcohol out of the football grounds, a relatively straightforward social control which is not difficult to enforce, the licence to express aggression in such an extreme form was removed. Nobody was being forbidden to drink; they were just not being allowed to take drink into the grounds. At baseball games in America, where beer is on sale in cardboard cups throughout the match, but where it is also forbidden to bring liquor into the stadium, violence is at a very low level. You can learn from this example, by removing yourself from those environments where you know that you tend to drink most heavily.

This is equally true for those who drink most heavily in public and those who drink most heavily in private. In both cases, you need to learn and practise self-control in the specific ways that have been suggested above. But you also need to take a broader view of your life and decide whether, by changing the places where you spend your leisure time or do your drinking, you can reduce the pressures on you to drink too much. It may mean staying at home more for some people; for others it may mean going out more.

For some of you it may even involve changing your job. Particular occupations are known to be associated with high alcohol damage rates. If alcohol is freely available to you at work or is subsidized in some way; if there is strong social pressure from your colleagues to drink heavily; if you are relatively free from supervision; and if your job means that you are quite mobile – if any or all of these factors apply, then there are forces at work which increase your risk of drinking more than is good for you. Obviously, changing your job is a dramatic step to take, but it would be foolish to ignore the fact that in some cases a working environment may be so hostile to a more moderate drinking style that there may be no alternative but to move. The four factors listed above – availability, social pressure, lack of supervision and increased mobility – are the ones you need to keep in mind when deciding whether a particular job is likely to have a good or bad effect upon your drinking.

Other dramatic changes in lifestyle might also be necessary in special circumstances. Somebody might have to move house because he lived in a village where the whole social life of the community centred upon the pub and where no alternative leisure activities existed. Generally, however, the vast majority of people are able to make choices about where they drink, as they can about when and how much they drink, without having to move or change jobs. But it is worth remembering that alcohol is so powerful a drug that some people have to take decisions of that kind in order to be able to win back control over their own lives. It does not mean that they are weak-willed people. Indeed, it must take a great deal of willpower to make so drastic a change. It simply means that alcohol is a substance which, both despite and because of the pleasure it brings, should never be taken lightly.

Choosing Your Friends

The people with whom you choose to drink are probably an even more important influence on your drinking style than when and where you drink. What you need to be sure of, first of all, is that they are indeed the people that you do actively *choose* to drink with, and not just the people with whom you have drifted into the habit of drinking. Once you recognize that their influence on your drinking may be an important reason for electing to spend time with one group of friends rather than another, you have already introduced another possible means of achieving a close control over your drinking style.

The basic principle involved is an obvious one. Try to spend more time with friends who drink less, and less time with friends who drink more. If some people are having an undesired effect on your drinking, then you need to ask yourself how important their friendship really is to you. Is it important enough to justify abandoning your attempt to avoid the drinking problems into which you have slipped?

Just as the drinking behaviour of your friends can influence you, so your own behaviour can influence that of the group. One faster drinker, for example, can force the pace of a whole group who are taking it in turns to buy rounds, since an empty glass on the table always makes the next person whose turn it is to buy feel guilty. If you are prepared to put into words what is likely to be the feeling of most of the rest of the group, then you are probably doing yourself and your fast-drinking friend a favour. A remark such as *'You bolted that one down pretty fast, didn't you?'* can help to establish a slower drinking style for the whole group.

It is also worth remembering that a group of friends is not something which is fixed for all time. If you feel that the people whose company you most enjoy are drinking rather more than they used to, try to introduce into the group some new individuals who drink less. Generally speaking, groups of friends which include both men and women will drink rather less than exclusively male groups of drinkers. You only have to think of the expression 'drinking mate' or 'drinking friend' to conjure up the picture, not just of somebody you drink with, but somebody you would be prepared to get drunk with. The idea that some friends might be reserved exclusively for drinking and excluded from other parts of your life should alert you to the possibility that time spent with those individuals is likely to be particularly hazardous for you. If you have chosen to get drunk with somebody in the past, then you are more likely to get drunk again with them than with somebody in whose company you have always remained fairly sober.

Although this section has been written about the friends with whom you choose to drink, the same principles obviously apply to other members of your family as well. Husbands and wives have a strong influence upon each other's drinking and parents have a strong influence upon the drinking behaviour of their children. Quite apart from the evidence of genetic factors in some kinds of alcoholic diseases, it is clear that heavy drinkers will often choose spouses who reinforce rather than challenge their habits. The children of heavy drinkers will tend either to drink quite heavily themselves or to be unusually hostile to what they perceive as excessive drinking.

Some people, of course, choose to drink alone. As has already been explained on pages 40 to 42, this is not necessarily in itself a danger sign, despite the popular myth. It is when solitary drinking is deliberately secretive, and when it is associated with other problems like depression or anxiety, that it is most likely to have unhealthy effects. If solitary drinking is stabilized at a low level of consumption, it need not be a cause for alarm; in the absence of other external controls, however, an upward consumption trend is particularly dangerous.

If you drink alone, but drink well within the safety margins described on pages 59 and 60, and if you are comfortable with that drinking style, then you do not need to be especially careful about monitoring the level and style of your consumption. If, however, you are uncomfortable about your drinking for any reason, then you might do well to try to find out what is troubling you and then take steps to change it. If, for example, it is the fact of being alone that is the problem, then the drinking will certainly do nothing to improve that. Resolving the problem of your loneliness will remove the anxieties about your drinking. Drinking more will only make you feel lonelier.

Gaining Confidence

Many of the strategies described in this section of the book have been concerned with helping you to gain the confidence to do what you want with your own life. They have, inevitably, been focused upon drinking behaviour. It must be obvious to you that confidence about your abilities to choose for yourself with regard to drinking is just part of being confident about yourself generally. But that principle works in both directions. If you are able to take more control of your drinking, then you will find that you are gaining control of other aspects of your life as well. Even small advances in your ability to achieve the drinking goals which you set for yourself will have important spin-off effects for the rest of your life. You will feel better about yourself, more confident, more certain that you can, after all, do what you want to do.

That is an important feeling and nothing to be ashamed about. It is even worth working on that feeling a bit more if you find that it is relatively short-lived or if it does not give you the satisfaction you had hoped for. Although not everybody who is using this book to help them avoid drinking problems will find this a worthwhile or necessary exercise, there are many for whom it will reinforce the gains they have made and give them added confidence to enable them to try other, possibly more difficult strategies. The exercise is based upon an extended version of the diary chart which appears on page 71. The idea which lies behind the exercise is that you will be better able to build upon your successes and

MONDAY	Alcohol consumption		Where and with whom
	TOTAL	GOAL	
Morning			
Lunchtime			
Afternoon			
Dinnertime			
Evening			
WHOLE DAY			

failures if you understand more about how they occurred. You can then analyse for yourself the factors which seem to be associated with success and which with failure, and emphasize the aspects of your drinking that have the strongest positive influence.

Reasons for drinking	Effects of drinking	What went right/wrong

MONDAY	Alcohol consumption TOTAL	Alcohol consumption GOAL	Where and with whom
Morning	*0*	*0*	
Lunchtime	*2*	*0*	*King's Head with Sarah.*
Afternoon	*0*	*1*	
Dinnertime	*3*	*2*	*At home with Arthur.*
Evening	*2*	*2*	*Crown and Greyhound with Arthur, Bill, Jane and Sarah.*
WHOLE DAY	*7*	*5*	

Reasons for drinking	Effects of drinking	What went right/wrong
Quite fancied a pint at about 11.45.	*Felt good about resisting the urge.*	*Forced myself to concentrate on difficult job.*
Sarah said she'd come to lunch with me. I know she always has a drink.	*Felt good about being with Sarah but angry at myself for drinking.*	*Didn't have the courage to order a soft drink. Stupid.*
Had promised myself half a pint on the way home. Decided not to.	*Felt virtuous.*	*Punishing myself for lunchtime. Is this healthy?*
We take it in turns to cook. Arthur always has a bottle of wine. I like two glasses.	*Helped the meal go down. Great.*	*Had one glass more than I'd intended. Never mind.*
Had planned to drink one pint. Stuck to it despite unexpected arrival of Sarah. Went on to coke. So did she.	*Talked to Sarah about drinking. She's on a health kick – admired my stand. Wow!*	*Decided on my limit and kept to it regardless. Was willing to talk about it.*

This inevitably involves a rather more elaborate kind of diary chart than those which have been illustrated previously. Although this diary, like the simpler versions, records both your goal (how much you intended to drink) and your total (how much you actually drank) it does so in the context of more information about the drinking situation. This version of your diary records the whole process of choosing to have a drink, your reasons, the effects and how you felt about it at the time. This is not the kind of diary chart which you can fill in surreptitiously. It takes time and its value for you will depend completely on the degree to which you are prepared to be honest with yourself. You also need to leave yourself enough space to write all you want. (*see pages 92 and 93*).

A diary chart like this can also be used to record information about how you felt when you chose *not* to have a drink. A fairly eventful 'drinking day' might, therefore, look something like the one shown on pages 94 and 95.

Despite the fact that he drank rather more than he had intended, it is clear that the man who filled in this diary learned some important lessons about his drinking.

Try this exercise out for a week or two and then look back over all the cards you have completed. You will almost certainly find some kind of pattern emerging from your experience. Particular sorts of situations may emerge as particularly difficult for you to deal with, and you can then plan ahead how to solve or, possibly, how to avoid them. Particular people, particular times of day or particular moods may all predict heavier drinking for you. Seeing a pattern emerge will help you to isolate those factors which you need to be wary of; it will also enable you to understand which circumstances helped you to control your drinking as you had planned. You can then use that information to extend the range of controllable situations and to achieve a greater level of consistency in your success at keeping within your limits.

Leisure Skills

For some people, whose drinking has been the most important thing in their social lives, it comes as a surprise to realize that there are ways of having a good time that do not involve alcohol. If a lot of your time has been spent with friends in the pub or sitting alone in front of your television set, and if you have found yourself drinking increasing amounts, it is likely that, in addition to all the strategies which have been described so far in this section of the book, you will want to find some alternative activities which are not associated with your previous lifestyle and which will help to strengthen your resolve to drink less. It is important to recognize that cutting down on the amount you drink will almost inevitably result in spending less time drinking. Unless you plan what you are going to do with that extra time, it is all too easy to end up bored, restless and frustrated, wondering whether the whole business was really such a great idea in the first place. In such a mood, the old crowd back in the pub may seem like a haven of refuge.

In order to avoid that dismal and self-defeating prospect, it is helpful to think of this extra spare time as an opportunity to take up new interests rather than a problem created by your loss of old pleasures. By thinking positively you are much more likely to make rewarding use of the chance to do something new. Remember, too, that it is not enough to do something worthy. You got pleasure out of your drinking. Make sure you get pleasure out of whatever you choose to do instead of drinking. It is, after all, most likely that you have not given up drinking completely. If you continue to enjoy evenings when you do have a drink more than those when you do not, then your brave new lifestyle is unlikely to last very long.

Although you can, of course, use your spare time to do anything you like, it is best to consider making a positive start on some specific new activity. Reading, watching television and going to the cinema are all satisfying ways of passing time, but they may be somewhat too general and passive to act as effective replacements for your drinking, especially if socializing was an important part of your drinking style. It is worth remembering that the decision to change your drinking behaviour was probably quite a radical one and may well have produced some kind of consequent stress for you, even if things are going relatively well. Choosing new leisure activities which are positively beneficial in terms of reducing that stress may therefore be a good idea and may help to underscore your successes.

Broadly speaking, leisure activities which involve physical exercise or mental relaxation are likely to be most effective as replacements for drinking. Even if you still go to the pub two or three times a week, you should be able to take up at least one activity from each category. Those involving physical exercise, which will help your body get back into shape if it has deteriorated because of your drinking, include activities like swimming, dancing, jogging, cycling, even walking. Those involving mental relaxation, which will help your mind come to terms with the consequences of your change in lifestyle, include activities like yoga, meditation, painting, or even having a regular sauna and massage. You may even need to take care that you do not become so fanatical about your new interests that you neglect to leave enough time for those aspects of your drinking that still give you real pleasure. You need to find a sense of balance in your use of leisure time.

Cost

In the section on long- and short-term effects of excessive drinking, the personal costs were discussed in terms of health and social consequences. There is, of course, another kind of cost as well. Drinking is an expensive activity.

Look back at the first diary chart that you filled in – the one which analysed your current drinking practice at the time when you began to read this book. Put a price to each drink that you consumed during that week and then add them all up. The total bill may be quite a lot larger than you had anticipated. Even if some of the drinks were bought for you by somebody else, it is sensible to cost out the week as if you had purchased each drink yourself at normal pub prices. If you still need further evidence of how expensive your drinking habits are, multiply that total by fifty-two to see how much it costs you per year. Compare the weekly total with your week's wages or the annual total with your annual salary. In either case, allow not just for income tax but for all the other fixed payments you have to make – things like rent, rates, mortgage, heating and lighting, basic food and clothing. Look at what proportion of the remainder you poured down your throat each week.

Now repeat the exercise, based upon your *new* drinking style. You may be pleasantly surprised to see how much money you are saving. Some people actually choose to put that sum (the difference between their old and their new drinking expenditure) into a special bank account each week. They say that it very soon mounts up into enough to take a special holiday or to make a down-payment on a new car. The importance of giving yourself rewards when you have reached your set goals has already been emphasized (see page 76). Here is an example of how, without even noticing it happening, you could give yourself a very substantial reward indeed.

Talking to Other People

The whole of this section has been about what you can do by yourself to improve your own drinking style so as to avoid unnecessary problems. Nothing has been suggested which actually *requires* the involvement of other people. You can do it by yourself.

If, however, there is somebody (a friend, a colleague, a member of your family) whom you really trust and in whom you feel confident, then a great deal can be gained by telling him what you are trying to do and asking him to help you. As much as anything else, his help will consist in the simple fact of being there. You will not want to let him down. More than that, however, he will be able to offer you support when you find things more difficult (which you will do from time to time) and encourage you if you sometimes fail to meet your own standards (which may well happen too). Having somebody with whom you can share the problems and the triumphs is likely to make the problems seem less difficult and the triumphs more important.

One possibility is to find somebody else who, like you, wants to cut down his drinking. Then you can offer each other support and encouragement on a mutual basis. Your commitment to succeed will be even greater because of your shared experiences.

Whether you take somebody else into your confidence or whether you try to accomplish the change yourself, you should remember one thing above all else: once you have decided that you really are going to transform your drinking style into how you want it to be, once you commit your energies and your sense of purpose, once you are willing to believe in your ability to succeed, then there is finally no earthly reason why you should do otherwise. If you have made your decision, if you have read this far, then you are already a lot closer to your goal than you realize.

4. HELPING OTHER PEOPLE

The main focus of this book so far has been on what people can do to improve their own drinking styles. However, it may not be your own drinking that concerns you, but that of somebody close to you. It may be a member of your family, a friend or a colleague. You want to find out whether there is anything you can do to help. You are anxious not to do the wrong thing, in case that might do more harm than good. This section of the book looks at the opportunities for you to intervene in somebody else's drinking. It assesses the range of strategies and indicates some of the pitfalls.

The first point to be made is that if you are worried that somebody close to you is drinking too much and if you feel that you are well placed, because of his* trust in you, to try to do something about it, then you should not spend too long agonizing about the ethics of the situation. Alcohol, as has been explained, is a powerful addictive drug. If somebody is becoming increasingly entangled in the meshes of addiction, then the longer you delay, the more difficult it is going to be to help him disentangle himself. While you are sorting out the rights and wrongs of whether you should do something, he is continuing to drink in a way which, if you are correct in your assessment of the situation, is harmful to him.

He may or may not recognize this. If there is something wrong with his drinking, then he may indeed be well aware of it himself, even if he is doing nothing specific to remedy the situation. He may be grateful that somebody cares enough for him to have noticed his problem and may welcome the help which you are offering. On the other hand, he may deny most vigorously that there is anything at all wrong with his drinking and may bitterly resent what he sees as your interference in his legitimate private pleasures. You really need to be prepared for either response, and

* The usage of the masculine pronoun in this book is adopted solely for convenience, and the reader should, of course, understand that wherever he/him/his is used, the alternative she/her should also be inferred.

for a range of intermediate positions, but remember that he will very likely not welcome your intervention with open arms.

Before you decide how you should first broach this subject with your partner or friend, it is important that you think very carefully about two sets of factors. You need to think in detail and using specific examples, not just vague impressions, about his drinking style. Use pages 29 to 47 to try to arrive at an accurate and objective view of the strengths and the weaknesses of the way he drinks. Do not start at this stage planning how you would like him to change. That is going to have to be a decision for him, not for you. What you need to have is a clear picture of *why* you want him to change.

That brings in the second factor you need to consider carefully. Although it is his own good that motivates you, you ought to recognize that you too have a vested interest in persuading him to change his drinking style. Perhaps he will be easier or more pleasant to live with, perhaps he will be a better friend or a better lover, more companionable or more reliable; perhaps he will be a more efficient colleague, or a better boss. Whatever you personally hope to gain by persuading him to change, it is essential that you admit it to yourself at this stage. Not only will it help you to deal more sensitively with the difficulties of self-assessment which will emerge for him; it will also mean that you have already had time to consider your response to the jibe which may well be thrown at you – *'You're doing this for yourself, not for me.'* If you have already considered that possibility, then you will be able to answer honestly – yes, you do stand to benefit from the change; but for *him* it is not just a matter of convenience or preference, but a matter of life and death.

Remember, before going any further, that nobody drinks in total isolation. The very fact that you are considering intervening in somebody else's drinking is an indication that it touches you. Usually, as we have already seen, someone's drinking style is strongly influenced by the behaviour of his friends. If your drinking style correlates with that of the person whom you want to change, then you are probably going to have to be prepared to do a bit of changing yourself in order to be of help. In taking the first step to reach an accurate and objective view of his drinking style, try also to get a sense of how it interacts with the styles of other people who are important to him, including yourself.

In order to gain a sense of what is actually involved in this process, it may be helpful once again to use a cluster of case histories. This time, however, as you read the accounts of these three members of a single family, notice not only what they say about their own drinking but also what they say (and do not say) about each other's.

LIZZIE (aged 38; married; housewife; one child)

'I've had time on my hands, so to speak, ever since Denise first went to school. That's nine years ago now. Mostly, it's no problem. I mean, I have a nice house, a car of my own, Tony's very generous, a good husband. But sometimes things really get me down. That's when I start hitting the bottle a bit hard.

'This time? It was that day in February when I ended up feeling there was nothing else left to go wrong. It began at lunchtime, driving back from town. This big Rover drove into me at a roundabout, his fault entirely, I mean I was actually stationary at the time. But it upset me and I forgot to do all the things I knew perfectly well I ought to have done. Forgot to grab a passing pedestrian as a witness. Forgot to insist on the police being called. Even forgot to take the registration number of his Rover. He must have thought he'd found a real sucker.

'I had my first one in the pub by the roundabout, as soon as he'd driven off leaving me. Just to steady my nerves, I told myself. A quick G and T. There was a big poster up advertising gin; you know, that wonderful green colour. Maybe that's what made me think of it in the first place. Anyway, I really enjoyed that first gin. So I had another. Then I went back to the car to find that I'd left it unlocked and somebody had stolen my stereo. It was all so stupid.

'Not so stupid as driving home and opening a bottle of sherry. By the time Denise got home from school, I'd gone through more than half of it. And I'd finished the rest before Tony came in at six. I could see he was angry, the way he looked at me. If only he'd just been sympathetic, said he understood, said he loved me, said it didn't matter. But, instead, he went all cold and distant, the way he does. He sent Denise down the road for a Chinese take-away. While she was out he started on at me, about letting myself go, about the mess I was in.

'It went on for hours, our argument. Denise ate her sweet and sour pork in silence, staring at us. Then she went up to her room. I don't think either of us said goodnight to her. I drank some more, too, during the evening. I think Tony had a few gins himself, actually. Then he said he was going to sleep in the spare room. So I stayed up, feeling life had reached its lowest ebb, drinking some more.

'I woke at about eleven the next day. Tony must have got Denise off to school. The house was like a grave. I felt dreadful. I couldn't face the rest of the day like that, alone, just waiting for them to come back, waiting for it all to begin again.

'So. Well, it seemed the easiest thing to do at the time. I'd plenty of money in my purse. I went down to the local supermarket and bought another bottle of gin and another bottle of sherry. Made myself look quite respectable for the occasion, said hullo to the neighbours.

'Don't get me wrong. I'm not an alcoholic. I mean, it sounds sordid, doesn't it, the way I describe it? But it's only occasionally it happens, only when something goes wrong, when I'm feeling low. It wouldn't take much to lift me out of it. Tony could do it, if he could be bothered. I admit this time was worse than usual. I don't know why. It's how I was, off and on, for three or four weeks, not always drunk, but never exactly sober. Denise hardly spoke to me and Tony still slept in the spare room. Not that it mattered much by that stage. I was drinking because I was drinking.

'It was my sister, who's married and lives in Basingstoke, who brought me back to my senses this time. I don't know whether Tony had telephoned her. I didn't like to ask. But anyway, she came round one afternoon when, fortunately, I wasn't too far gone. We had a long talk. I told her about everything. My marriage, I mean, it's not ideal, but whose is nowadays? Well, she was sympathetic but very firm. Made me promise. No more booze. And it wasn't all that difficult to stop. That's why I say I'm not an alcoholic. It's not the drink that's the problem. It's the problems that make me drink.'

TONY (aged 42; married; salesman; one child)

'It's not my problem, it's my wife's. Don't get me wrong. I like a drink. Who doesn't? But in moderation. Anyway, in my line of work, you can't be too careful. Have one over the eight and it's not difficult

for somebody to pull the wool over your eyes. You'd be surprised how many try.

'In my opinion, Lizzie's just let herself go. I mean, she was really attractive once, when I married her, but I bet the building workers don't whistle at her now. Know what I mean? I'm not being nasty. Just stating facts. And she's aware of it, in my opinion, aware of losing her looks, so there's a kind of desperation about her sometimes. And that's when she starts on one of her drinking bouts.

'They're more frequent now than they used to be. The first one, I'll never forget it, was six years ago now, when she found out about the affair I was having with a woman at the office. So, I grant you she had an excuse that time. Maybe other times too. But, somehow, the excuses seem to get easier and easier every time.

'This last one, it was a car crash. Nothing serious, you see, just a dented tailgate and rear light assembly. Not even her fault, but it was enough. By the time I got home from work she was virtually incoherent. What angered me most was that Denise – she's our fourteen-year-old – was sitting there watching television in the same room. It's not right that Lizzie should show herself up in front of the girl. It's not fair on her. It's not fair on me.

'I tried to keep calm about it. I tried to keep my feelings to myself. I just sent Denise out to get a take-away from the Chinese restaurant. I told Lizzie she had to pull herself together. But then she started in at me. Again. Raking over old coals, going on and on about things that were dead and buried between us.

'I have to confess I needed a drink by then myself. And Lizzie used it as an excuse to start in again too. In the end I just went off to the spare room, leaving her down there holding on to the gin bottle as if she expected me to tear it out of her hand.

'It was a month this time. Sometimes it's less, sometimes it's more. I can't do anything when she's like that. She won't listen to reason. In the end I got her sister to come over. I hate doing that because I feel it's like admitting defeat. Admitting that we can't work out our own problems. But it's Denise I think of. I have to keep things on an even keel for her sake. And anyway, when she's not hitting the bottle, Lizzie can be good company. I mean many's the time we've gone off to the pub together or out for a meal.

'Maybe it's partly my fault. Maybe I should have spent more

time with her. But my job takes me away a lot. Anyway, I think it's mostly to do with Lizzie herself. I wonder if it's her time of life, you know what I mean, though maybe she's a bit young for that. Not that you'd think so to look at her.'

DENISE (aged 14; schoolgirl)

'I really hate my parents. I wish I didn't. I wish I was like other girls, I mean having arguments with them and all that, but loving them really, and being loved.

'But it's not like that in our house. I sometimes wonder if they really wanted me in the first place. They certainly don't seem to want me now.

'They seem to argue all the time. Sometimes it's just awful and other times it's unbearable. It used to upset me a lot but since I've come to realize that I hate them, it's been easier just to shut it off. I don't know why they ever got married, except that each is as bad as the other. They deserve each other.

'Then I sometimes wonder what I'm supposed to have done to deserve them. But that's stupid thinking, isn't it? I mean, there's no such thing as God, is there? You only have to look at my RE teacher to realize that.

'Mum drinks, of course, and so does Dad, though not so much. Or maybe he just holds it better. When Mum's been drinking, she looks all sort of sloppy and puffy and she speaks as if she's not sure what the words really sound like. She never cooks or anything when she's been drinking and she doesn't wash either.

'Sometimes Dad shouts at her, sometimes he just stares and says nothing. I've never seen him hit her, but I bet he wants to. What he does is to take it out on me. For the slightest thing. I mean, I'm fourteen and he treats me like a kid. He gave me a hiding last weekend because I came in at ten o'clock from the school disco. It wasn't my fault. It didn't even finish till nine-thirty and I had to wait for Sammy. If he cared so much, he could have come and fetched me like the other dads, couldn't he?

'I've tried it myself, drinking. When Mum's like that, she wouldn't notice how much is left in the bottle. I don't like sherry much but gin is all right. It's sort of thicker than water, do you know what I mean, and perfumey. Like drinking the cosmetic counter at John Lewis's.

I felt a bit sick the first time, but I'm used to it now. I've got to be careful Dad doesn't find out. He'd kill me if he knew.

'I stay in my room more and more. I listen to records, well, tapes really, which I record off the radio. I know the words of all the songs in the top twenty off by heart. What I like best in the world is just lying in bed, listening to really great music, with some of Mum's gin hidden under the bedclothes and hearing them, just faintly, arguing with each other downstairs. That way, I know I'm better than them.

'I'd like it to be different. I'd like to be able to invite friends home. But how can I? I never know if she's going to be sober. Or if he's going to be in one of his moods.

'It'll never change. How can it? I can hardly wait till I'm old enough to leave home. I want to be a receptionist.'

The Right Person at the Right Time

In their different ways, Lizzie, Tony and Denise all need help, yet they seem curiously incapable of helping each other. Let us say that, for the time being, it is Lizzie's drinking which most urgently requires outside assistance. It is clear that neither Tony nor Denise are currently in the best position to help – Denise because she is too inexperienced, Tony because he remains judgemental and unsympathetic. It is, in fact, Lizzie's sister (involved, but at a distance) who is able to break into the vicious circle of her drinking. And by Lizzie's own admission, the timing may have been important too, since 'she came round one afternoon when, fortunately, I wasn't too far gone'.

There are several important lessons to be learned here. Firstly, it is wrong to assume that the person closest to the drinker is necessarily the one best placed to offer help. There may even be times when advice would be rejected if it were offered by a spouse or partner. Advice often seems less threatening if it comes from somebody less intimately involved. Remember that people can be very sensitive about what they perceive as criticism of their drinking. Some men may interpret it as an insult to their manhood; some women may feel that it represents an unwarranted intrusion into their private affairs. The closer you are to somebody, the more your criticism of him can hurt and, though you may have intended only to help, he may view it as an attack.

So ask yourself whether you are the best person to intervene. Is there somebody else, maybe somebody at work or another member of the family, whom you can trust and whose advice, for whatever reason, is more likely to seem acceptable? Do not feel that you have failed if you come to the conclusion that you are not the best person to speak to him about his drinking. On the other hand, do not ask somebody else to do it for you just because it seems too awkward or difficult. In the case above, Tony probably did the right thing in asking Lizzie's sister to help, but it is clear from what Lizzie says that Tony could have helped her himself in a far more fundamental way if he had been prepared to be rather more open and sympathetic at an earlier stage.

This leads on to the second lesson, which has to do with timing. It was a crisis which started Lizzie's drinking bout off in the first place. Thus it needed some positive action to startle her out of the pattern of destructive drinking into which she had slipped. There are no easy rules about judging the right moment to intervene except that, in general terms, it is not advisable to keep procrastinating in the hope that things will improve of their own accord: they usually do not.

Sometimes it is possible to make use of a drink-related event in the drinker's life for your first move. If, for example, he has nearly run someone over when driving home drunk from the pub, you may be able to use the incident to shock him into an awareness of the danger which his drinking is causing – to himself and to others. It is important, however, to make sure that you use an incident which has genuinely startled or upset him and not just one which has troubled you. If he arrives home drunk at three o'clock in the morning and wakes up the baby, that may make you upset and angry but seem quite trivial to him. To use that sort of incident as a way of opening up a discussion about his drinking is likely to end up in an acrimonious slanging match.

It is, in any case, bad policy to try to talk to people about their drinking when they are actually drunk. They may argue more in these circumstances, or they may appear wonderfully compliant, but you can be sure that their reaction, whatever it is, will change when they sober up. Apart from anything else, it is quite possible that they will not even remember the incident and they will certainly not feel bound by any promises which they made when drunk.

If you have decided that you are the best person to talk to your friend or partner about his drinking, choose a time when you are going to be alone together undisturbed for long enough to have a reasonable discussion. It may be that he does not particularly want to talk right away, but if he does, the last thing you want is to have to interrupt him. Find somewhere reasonably private, where you both feel at ease. Do not engineer a completely artificial situation, or it is likely that he will feel that you are manipulating him and will not feel like discussing his problem.

Remember, finally, in deciding the right moment and in choosing the right words, that if you find the occasion difficult, it is going to be a great deal more difficult for him. However tactfully you handle it, you are exposing something which he has previously kept hidden. Even if he welcomes your intervention, he is still going to be hurt. So, whatever his immediate response, accept it, if only for the time being. Avoid self-righteousness at all costs.

Confrontation, Threats and Insinuation

You are not a therapist. Do not make the mistake of trying to take charge of somebody else's problems. You are simply helping him come to terms with the consequences of his drinking and, if he is willing, to start a process of change. The last thing you want is for him to come to rely upon you as a crutch. He must learn to rely on himself.

It is all too easy to be seduced, particularly if things are going well, into the feeling that it is all because of your dedication and skill. Forget it. If he is succeeding in his aims, then it must be because *he* is making the changes, not because you are always there behind him. Of course, your support is important, but only to teach him how to cope on his own. It is at your peril that you over-estimate your own capacities in such a relationship. Do not forget that you have never received formal training in how to deal with the really difficult problems that may be surfacing. What you do have is concern, sympathy and a will to help. All those, and common sense. It is a formidable armoury, but you need to be acutely aware of your limits.

There is no way, for example, that Lizzie's sister is going to be able to resolve Lizzie's self-doubts and depression, Tony's alienation and anger, their fragile marriage and the even more precarious mental state of their daughter Denise. All Lizzie's sister can hope to do is to start something which will have possible benefits in all those areas. That is why the way the start is made is so important.

It has already been suggested that one way to make the first move is to use opportunities which arise out of the adverse consequences of drinking. That is a technique which has both advantages and disadvantages. Much may depend upon the attitude you project towards the problem, and that in turn will depend upon your relationship with the drinker. It is probably a good idea to be as straightforward as possible, firm but not aggressive, brief but not curt. If you make your approach too ambiguous, you may end up never having said what you really wanted to and having lost an opportunity which may not come again for a long time.

It is, after all, possible to be clear without being brutal. On the other hand, some element of confrontation is almost inevitable in whatever approach you make, simply because you are going to walk into an area of someone's life that was previously fenced off as private. How open are you prepared to be in that confrontation? That can only be a matter of individual judgement, based upon the quality of your relationship and the nature of the problems with which you are dealing.

One thing, however, is certain: if you make threats, you must be prepared to carry them out. There is no point in saying: *'Unless you cut down on your drinking, I'm going to leave you,'* if you both know that you have absolutely no intention of putting that threat into practice. In those circumstances, you are just playing a foolish and potentially dangerous game of collusion, which is likely to leave you both frustrated and disappointed. All-or-nothing threats of that sort are generally self-defeating. On the other hand, more limited threats can operate as an extension of the reward and punishment system described on page 76.

'I don't like being with you in public when you've had too

much to drink. Next time you do that, I'm just going to walk out of the restaurant and take a taxi home.'

That is a workable threat, because it is not too extreme. It relates to a specific piece of alcohol-related behaviour and it will not actually cause you more distress to carry it out than not to do so. If you have to use such a 'punishment', you also have to be prepared to hand out due 'rewards' as well.

'I really enjoyed being with you tonight. You kept to your limits beautifully. Listen, let me pay the bill.'

Remember, therefore, that threats are double-edged weapons. If the drinker calls your bluff, do not allow yourself to be forced into doing something which is actually to your own disadvantage. Apart from anything else, it will confirm for him that he has more power over you than you do over him.

Often, a process of insinuation may be more tactically effective than confrontation, provided that you do not allow it to obscure your basic message. The point is that everybody's drinking style is influenced by a number of potent factors – the drinking style of his friends, the amount of money he wants to spend on drinking, images of drinking on television and in advertising, and so on. You can use these influences as ways of imparting a healthier value system:

'That friend of yours, Bob, you know, he looked really stupid last night. Did you notice, he kept letting beer spill out of his mouth? And he thought he was so sexy, didn't he? People don't realize how pathetic they look when they've had too much to drink.'

You can use statements like that to imply your position without actually needing to state it explicitly. Similarly, if you are prepared to include yourself in the implied criticism, you can make a vivid point using the simple factor of cost:

'I've just worked it out. Do you know, with what you and I spent last night in the pub, we could actually have bought four LPs/gone to Paris on the boat-train/afforded tickets for that concert.'

The alternative must, of course, seem even more attractive than a jolly evening in the pub, otherwise the point is lost. Nor should you nag or your criticism is likely to be deliberately ignored.

Even advertising can be used, at least in a negative sense.

'Do you think anybody's fooled by that? Being successful has

got nothing to do with drinking that stuff. I bet I could not drink at all for a week/a fortnight/a month and it wouldn't make any difference to how I made out.'

Again, you may have to be prepared to put yourself on the line by volunteering to abstain temporarily, in order to help him on his way. The point about a mutual period of temporary abstinence is, of course, that it enables you to gain a sense of his degree of dependence upon alcohol by comparing how difficult you each find it to do without drink. It is sometimes easier to start a new set of drinking habits, to establish a new drinking style, if there has been a real gap which separates the new from the old. The temptation just to slip back into old ways is likely to be less strong if, after a week or two of not drinking at all, he then starts to drink again in a different way, with different people or in a different place. Help him to make a completely fresh start.

Being Willing to Talk

This means both of you. The chances are that if you are going to get anywhere in helping somebody to reassess his drinking style, you will both have to do some frank talking. And, especially in your own case, some careful listening. Once you have started the ball rolling by making the first move, you have a responsibility to stay with it until it comes to rest.

Here, the case of Lizzie is especially helpful. Although her sister could hardly expect to solve Lizzie's problems, she certainly had to be prepared to hear about them. *'We had a long talk. I told her everything. My marriage, I mean, it's not ideal . . .'* and so on. If somebody has a problem to do with their drinking, then it is almost certain that he will have other problems as well. He may even believe, as Lizzie does, that it is the other problems which cause the drinking problem. And he may be right about that. The point is that by lifting the lid on the drinking problem, you are allowing all the other problems to be ventilated too. Just by listening sympathetically, you may be doing more than you realize. At the same time, if he is revealing confidences to you, he may expect to hear something from you in return. Not that it should be a competition in which you strive to prove that you are in an even bigger mess than he is; you should merely say enough to reassure him that you trust him as he trusts you. It is, at its simplest, a way of establishing your credentials. Not as a therapist, remember, just as a true friend.

Once you have got past that particular phase, you may find that it will be possible, using pages 29 to 47 of this book as a guide, to reassess his drinking style with him. Look at the different variables; talk about the factors that seem to be associated with particularly heavy drinking episodes. Begin to discuss how it might be possible to change those factors so as to reduce the likelihood of excessive drinking. It may at this stage even be helpful to suggest to him that he should read the section of this book on avoiding drinking problems (pages 65 to 100). This will give him a sense of what he can achieve through his own efforts. So (you can argue), with your help, is it not going to be worth putting some effort into it? The benefits, at this stage, need to look substantial.

Reinforcing the Decision

There is no way that you can legitimately make somebody else's decisions for him. If he is going to change the way he drinks, then he is going to need to learn and practise his own decision-making skills in the way that is described on pages 66 to 68. What you can do is to recognize that the decisions he makes demand decisions from you as well.

Lizzie's sister persuades her not to drink for a time and Lizzie is prepared to go along with that plan. She will stand a much better chance of being successful if Tony changes his behaviour too; not just his drinking behaviour, although that in itself will be important, but also, in more general terms, his behaviour to his wife: she is going to need much more attention during this difficult phase. To judge by Denise's description of their marriage, that will involve a major adjustment on Tony's part. Just as the ripples of Lizzie's drinking spread out until they seem capable of swamping the whole family, so the fundamental changes when she cuts out drinking will have a direct impact upon her husband and daughter. What will happen to Denise's habit of stealing her mother's gin when there is no gin there to steal? It is possible, given a willingness by the others to adjust in their own ways, that

Lizzie's change of drinking style will radically improve the quality of family life, even in unanticipated ways.

Not every change will seem desirable either. While you may have resented the time the drinker wasted in the pub, you may not welcome him hanging around home every evening. It is especially important at this stage not to give in to an impulsive surge of anger. *'For goodness sake, stop mooning about like that. You were more fun when you were drinking,'* is an open invitation to throw over all that has been achieved and start again on the spiral of damaging drinking. Same again. Do not make the mistake of thinking that you could not possibly be so insensitive as to say such a thing. Changing a drinking style means changing a whole way of life and it is only to be expected that there will be some anger and bitterness along the way. You, at least, can have taken the step of working out beforehand where the dangers are most likely to occur and how you plan to cope with them. You may even find it helpful to make a chart, writing down the changes you expect him to make in one column, the changes you think you will therefore have to make in another and then, thirdly, any difficulties that you think may arise. The result might look something like this:

Planned change (him)	*My change*	*Difficulty*
1. To the pub less frequently.	Spend evenings together.	Not used to each other's company.
2. Spend less on drink.	More money for me?	Is that really fair?
3. Go jogging each morning.	Go jogging together.	I find jogging boring.

Face up to the difficulties and they will seem less disruptive than if they take you by surprise. You can use this exercise to help reinforce the changes the drinker is making by demonstrating that you, too, are involved in the process of change, even if the primary responsibility is his.

You can also help to monitor (with or without this exercise) how successfully he is keeping to the limits or goals he set for himself. If you help him set these limits, then make sure that you do not force him into accepting unrealistic goals he has no hope of achieving. Indeed, as far as possible, encourage him to set his own limits, because otherwise, if he does fail, he can always blame you for having persuaded him against his will. He can even use your involvement as an excuse to justify a lapse. Similarly, in helping to monitor how well he is doing, your role should be that of a father-confessor rather than that of a policeman.

In this context, it is worth remembering that there are occasions when it may be perfectly reasonable for somebody to drink more than he usually allows himself, provided that such occasions are infrequent and provided that he acknowledges beforehand that this is an exception he is making deliberately. It is not something to be decided after the event. However, all rules need not be thrown to the winds. You can help him set other, more relaxed limits for that particular occasion and you can remind him of those limits if he seems in danger of forgetting them.

Another way in which you can help to reinforce his decisions is to be very selective in the remarks which you make about drinking in general. Although the basic philosophy of this book is that, properly used, alcohol does more good than harm, it is clear that, if somebody needs to change his drinking style, it must currently be doing him more harm than good. The section on short- and long-term effects of excessive drinking described some of the kinds of harm that may be involved (see pages 51 to 61). It is quite likely that, as somebody begins to try to change, he will keep being reminded of all the good things that drinking represents to him. Remember that the list of reasons for continuing (page 67) is going to seem very persuasive indeed. *You*, therefore, can play the part of the other voice. You can reinforce all the negative aspects of drinking – the costs to his pocket and to his health; the risks – to himself and to others. And you can deliberately ignore the positive aspects of drinking. In doing this it is important that you do not come to seem like a kill-joy. You should remain calm and reasonable throughout, stating facts without whining or nagging or hectoring. While all this may be infuriating if it is carried to an extreme, if it is used judiciously it can simply act as a reinforcement of the decision he has already made for himself.

Removing Temptation

It is never going to be possible (even if it was desirable) to remove temptation entirely, but you can help by making the environment more supportive of the decision the drinker has made. If one of the decisions was that he would cut out the glass of whisky he always used to have as soon as he got in from work, then not only should you be prepared to cut out your gin and tonic, but you might also think it worthwhile putting the bottles away in the sideboard rather than having them sitting on top. You should perhaps ban those three-litre wine boxes from the fridge, so that the temptation to have 'just one more glass' will be minimized. You should make sure that there are plenty of soft drinks, mineral water and milk around so that, if he feels like a drink, it does not necessarily have to be alcohol. You can develop a taste for special blends of tea or coffee and make sure there is always a good variety in the cupboard.

It is important, of course, not to carry this principle too far. If you find that you have reached the stage of locking away the booze and hiding the key, then maybe both of you require treatment.

What has been described here with regard to the home environment is equally true for the working environment. If you are assisting a colleague to cut down drinking, then he should not be the one to have the drinks cabinet in his office. Alternatively, you can probably get him to agree 'for security reasons' to lock it and give the key to his secretary to keep in his or her desk. That way, while he is not denied access to the cabinet, he has to go to some trouble to open it, thus reducing the chances of an impulsive swig after a difficult telephone call.

Going out to non-licensed restaurants at lunchtime does not necessarily mean confining yourself to ghastly food. Check out the establishments near your work. Make sure that when you eat sandwiches for lunch at work you do not automatically have a beer at the same time. If somebody is trying to cut down, they are going to be taking their cues from you. If drinking at lunchtime is not good for them, how come you believe yourself to be immune?

These factors become all the more important when you

find yourself in the role of host. There are some general lessons here as well: always provide non-alcoholic beverages as well as alcohol; don't go round topping up people's glasses all the time; stop serving alcohol well before the end of the social occasion and provide tea and coffee at that time instead. These are good rules to observe anyway, but they become especially important if you are actually helping somebody to cut down on their drinking. It is not generous to behave like a drug-pusher.

Providing Support

Of all the different things which you, as a friend, can do to help somebody change his drinking style, the most important is probably the least dramatic. Simply by being available, in person or at the end of a telephone, you can probably do a lot more than you imagine. Make sure that he understands that you mean it when you say that you do not mind being contacted whenever he feels he needs somebody to talk to. Make sure that *you* understand what that means, too: he may need to have a talk at a time which is not the most convenient for you. Here, too, you must tread a careful path between being easily accessible so that he feels comfortable in approaching you, but not so much at his beck and call that he starts to exploit your good nature.

One important aspect of this support is to provide reassurance when something has gone wrong, to confirm that one slip does not mean the end of the road. There will be setbacks – that is inevitable, and your support, generous, fair and level-headed, will be an important factor in rekindling the belief that he can, indeed, still achieve his self-appointed goals. Do not be so forgiving that he feels it scarcely matters that he has failed, but it is important that you should be sympathetic so that he is willing to continue to trust you.

This objective but concerned view is the kind of support which you can give in especially difficult times. But the day-to-day support which comes simply from being a part of the efforts he is making is just as important. If you feel that this is tending to fade into the background and become less significant than it should be, then there are several ways in which you can make your involvement rather more specific and precise, and which will emphasize its importance to him as well.

Take, for example, the expanded version of the diary chart shown on pages 92 and 93. You can arrange for your friend to discuss progress with you at the end of each week, bringing together the seven cards that have been filled in and looking at them for patterns of events. In discussion with you, trends which he might never have noticed for himself may well emerge. You can offer comments and suggestions for ways of overcoming difficulties.

If you are present yourself at most of his drinking occasions, then you can keep a parallel diary to his, comparing the two narratives at the end of each week. Although this is likely to make him rather self-conscious about his drinking, that is probably, on balance, a good thing: one of the main purposes of the techniques described in this book is to try to suggest to people that they should take their drinking less for granted.

Another, rather more elaborate exercise may be worth undertaking if you really do feel a long-term commitment to help bring about change. Get your friend to write a description of his behaviour (especially in relation to drinking, but taking other factors into account as well) before he began to try to change. This description should be a fair assessment, as he sees it, of his strengths and weaknesses and should include the reasons he had at the time for choosing to behave as he did. You should write a description of how you saw him at that same time, also trying to be as fair and objective as possible. Do not compare the two portraits yet. Wait until you both feel that some real and consistent changes are occurring, then repeat the exercise, describing on this occasion the different lifestyle which has now emerged. As you compare all four portraits, some important lessons are bound to emerge. If he feels that all this is rather unfair on him, there is no reason why the exercise should not be applied to you as well. Maybe that way, you will benefit from the changes in your friend's drinking in ways that you had never expected.

The importance of taking up new and invigorating leisure pursuits was emphasized in pages 96 to 97. You can play an important part in making these activities seem worthwhile and enjoyable by joining in yourself. It is sometimes difficult to go to some new club or class alone as an absolute beginner. If two of you go together, it can seem a great deal less threatening. On the other hand, remember to leave your friend enough space to do things alone. He may not always want you around. Learn to respect his sense of independence as a sign of his growing self-reliance.

Rejection, Failure and the Next Time Around

With the best will in the world, not everybody who tries to help a friend with his drinking is going to succeed. Enough has already been said in this book about difficulties. It does not matter what words are used to describe it all: lack of insight, low motivation, immaturity, addiction. The fact of the matter is that some people are likely to resist most strongly the suggestion that they need to do anything about their drinking.

In the end, if they persist in that opinion, you have no option but to accept it, at least for the time being. How you react to the rejection of an offer of help depends on what kind of offer it was and in what terms it was rejected. Unless something has gone far wrong, there is no reason why the rejection should destroy the relationship between you. It will alter it, certainly; you cannot expect just to go on as if nothing had happened. But, with luck and with tact (especially on your part), there is no reason why you should not still have a sound basis for friendship. And maybe, sometime in the future, the seed sowed by your words will bear fruit. Be prepared for a long wait, but, if you value the relationship, do not just accept a single rejection as the end of the story.

There are also going to be some people who fail. The trouble with failure is that it makes people want to apportion blame. This is such a complex area of life that blame is never going to rest with one person. If, despite everything, Lizzie starts to drink again, who is to say it would be her fault? Might it not equally be Tony's? Or even Denise's? So, if it seems that things are going badly, try not to think of it as a failure. Try to pick up the pieces and start again. You will have learned something along the way and will probably be even better equipped to help than you were previously.

Do not pretend that it does not matter. Of course it matters;

it matters a great deal. But it is not, or need not be, the final word, not even if the failure seems to have involved a catastrophe. Many people who finally succeed in changing their drinking styles have tried again and again before they felt that they had achieved the lifestyle they wanted. By recognizing when things go badly, by trying to see what went wrong so as to prevent that happening again, what you are doing is working against failure. There is, in that sense, no such thing as failure, only delayed success. And the scope for delay is the length of your patience.

Patience is a hard virtue to practise. Remember that it does not mean a willingness to be exploited. You are a person in your own right, a person with your own rights. Your patience has to do with a recognition that, because changing drinking styles is not easy, you do not expect immediate success. You care enough to wait around for the next time. Then, if next time is the same again, you will still be there, just so long as you can be sure that your friend believes in what he is trying to do.

Drinking Careers

Years ago the view of alcoholism was that people had to reach rock bottom before they could be helped. But evidence from sources all around the world has now made it clear that many people with alcohol problems can be helped very much earlier. Indeed, the earlier an intervention occurs, the more likely it is that help will prove effective. That fact is fundamental to the approach advocated by this book.

There is, however, one other basic concept which is also relevant – the concept of drinking careers. People do not always drink in exactly the same way for the whole of their lives. There are particular periods in many people's lives when they happen to drink more heavily than at others. For example, young men between the ages of eighteen and twenty-five are often in the position of having relatively high incomes and few responsibilities. It is, therefore, a time when they tend to drink quite heavily and some of them get into difficulties as a result of their drinking – difficulties like fights, accidents, minor trouble with the law. Most drunk driving convictions come from this age group. It is clear that most of these young men are going to change their drinking styles as they grow older and take on more responsibilities. Nobody tells them they are alcoholics and nobody forces them to change. It occurs spontaneously.

Similarly, later in life, a period of heavier drinking sometimes follows bereavement and, after the passing of the worst of the pain, a more moderate pattern of drinking usually reasserts itself. The point here is simply to note that the person whose drinking is causing you concern may be going through a heavier drinking phase which actually needs, in a sense, to be weathered. You can help, you can offer support and advice, but in the end it may be that they are going to have to grow as individuals in order to come out the other side of the drinking.

By contrast, there are periods in people's lives when they certainly ought not to be drinking very much at all. In the family case history given earlier in this section, it is probably Denise's secret drinking which is the most worrying single problem. A fourteen-year-old girl drinking gin alone to cope with her sense of despair is, by anybody's standards, an extremely serious mental and social problem. Indeed, anybody who is drinking in order to relieve severe symptoms of depression or anxiety is almost certainly in need of urgent professional help.

Another time when heavy drinking (and some would say any drinking) is harmful is during pregnancy. Growing evidence points to the dangers of damage to the unborn child as a result of even quite low levels of alcohol consumption. Similarly, there are occupations, particularly those associated with public transportation, military operations, medical practice, indeed any job where other people's lives are at risk, which are incompatible with heavy drinking.

Thus, drinking careers run throughout people's lives, with humps and troughs, hills and valleys, times of raised risk and times of lowered risk. In assessing whether you ought to intervene, you need to try to think of their drinking in the context of what you know about the whole of their lives. This is especially relevant because of another parallel concept – the natural history of alcohol addiction. Remember that alcohol is a powerful addictive drug and that many people who go on taking it without any thought for its consequences may find that their dose creeps up gradually, imperceptibly, over the years. That is why it is worth your while trying to do something. Because, if you do not, the chances are that things will deteriorate further: if you are wrong, little has been lost; if you are right, you may have saved a life.

5. SOURCES OF FURTHER HELP

Whether you have been trying to change your own drinking or somebody else's, it is possible that, having tried everything suggested in this book, you really feel that you have made no progress. Or you may feel that the problems you are concerned about are too deadly to warrant trying to deal with them yourself. For medical reasons or because you believe somebody's life (your own or another person's) is at risk, you may feel that you need to seek professional help.

If so, you should do something about it straight away. The longer you leave it, the worse these problems will be, the greater the risks. Do not promise yourself that you will do something about it tomorrow. Do it today.

Self, Family and Friends

This book has been about what you can do yourself and what you can expect of your family and friends. This is a powerful set of resources. Even if you do decide to seek outside help, that does not mean that you should abandon the help you can receive from your inner resources and from the concern of those close to you. The support which you can gain from these resources is going to be of immense importance in reinforcing whatever else happens. The people who do best in treatment are invariably those whose family and friends support them and who have confidence in themselves.

Self-help Groups

The most famous of all agencies in the alcohol world is, of course, Alcoholics Anonymous. AA is a self-help fellowship which has provided a way back to sobriety for countless people with alcohol problems. Not everybody who tries AA does well there, but for those who find it helpful, it can become the central focus of their lives. AA headquarters in Britain will provide lists of groups throughout the country. You should contact:

Alcoholics Anonymous,
UK General Services Office,
PO Box 514,
11 Redcliffe Gardens,
London, SW10
TELEPHONE: 01–352 9779

Anybody who believes he has a drinking problem and who seriously wants to do something about it is welcome to attend an AA meeting. If you do not want to contact the General Office in London, you can usually find a contact number for your local group in your telephone directory.

Associated with AA is another organization known as Al-Anon, which provides group support for the relatives and friends of alcoholics. Like AA, Al-Anon has groups throughout the country, and their headquarters are at:

Al-Anon Family Groups UK,
61 Dover Street,
London, SE1 4YF
TELEPHONE: 01–403 0888

Al-Ateen, which is intended for the adolescent children of alcoholics, can also be contacted through that address.

AA, Al-Anon and Al-Ateen all focus upon the alcoholic, that is to say the alcohol addict whose life has been severely damaged by drinking. As yet, relatively few self-help groups exist for those whose drinking problems are at an earlier stage. However, there is one called Drinkwatchers, which is now beginning to expand; it offers a group support system based upon self-monitoring principles similar to those described in this book. At present, Drinkwatchers is relatively limited geographically, but can be contacted at:

Accept Services UK,
Western Hospital,
Seagrave Road,
London, SW6 1RZ
TELEPHONE: 01–281 3155

In general terms, the advantages of any self-help approach to alcohol problems is that you can be sure that the other people there really do share the problems which you are experiencing. That strong sense of group identity is, for many people, a crucial factor in finding the road to health and happiness.

Advice Centres

There has been a rapid growth during the 1970s of local advice centres based in the communities which they serve. Although some of these are run by social services departments, most are voluntary bodies, offering a range of different services. Those called Local Councils on Alcoholism usually provide information, counselling and referral services, although there is some variation in approach, depending upon the strengths of particular councils. They are all affiliated to:

Alcohol Concern (National Agency on Alcohol Misuse),
3 Grosvenor Crescent,
London, SW1X 7EL
TELEPHONE: 01–235 4182

Information can be obtained from that source about whether there is a Local Council on Alcoholism in your area and also about other local services for those with alcohol problems. Comparable information about services in Scotland can be obtained from:

The Scottish Council on Alcoholism,
147 Blythwood Street,
Glasgow, G2 4EN
TELEPHONE: 041–333 9677

Some form of community level service exists in most areas. All are confidential and will certainly include sympathetic and informed advice. A telephone call will confirm whether you need to make an appointment or whether you can simply turn up at the centre.

Doctors and Clinics

Your own general practitioner is a possible source of immediate help. Your GP, with his knowledge of your past medical history, may be able to do a great deal to help you without having to refer you on to a specialist of any kind, particularly if your drinking problem is not too far advanced. Bear in mind, however, that GPs often think of alcoholics as rather demanding patients who require a great deal of time and effort. Try to reassure your GP of your willingness to cooperate and your intention not to place too great a burden upon him. Most GPs nowadays are coming to recognize that there is little point in replacing addiction to alcohol with addiction to prescribed drugs, so you should not expect that you will receive extended doses of tranquillizers from him. There are, however, some drugs which can assist in the early stages of alcohol withdrawal and there are others which can be used to back up a commitment to total abstinence.

If your GP is of the opinion that your alcohol problem is so severe that you require hospital treatment, you may be referred to an alcoholism treatment unit. These units are usually situated in psychiatric hospitals and have both in-patient and out-patient programmes. Alternatively, it is possible that, after tests, your GP will find that some particular organ of your body, such as your liver, is so badly damaged that you need to go to a general medical hospital for treatment.

Usually, referral to hospital can only be through your GP, and few clinics will accept you for treatment if you simply turn up on the doorstep. Your GP will also be able to provide you with information on private clinics if you feel that the facilities of the National Health Service are not for you.

Where Else to Turn

For one reason or another, you may feel that none of the specialist sources of help listed above is suitable for you. If so, there are other people to whom you can turn. There are, for example, other advice services, such as the Samaritans and the Marriage Guidance Council, whose emphasis is not so much upon the drinking as upon problems (despair, loneliness, marital stress) which you feel may be the cause of your drinking. Their telephone numbers will be in your local directory. Some social service departments also run or help to coordinate community advice centres in their locality.

Even if you are not a regular churchgoer, you may feel that a priest or minister of religion will be the best person to give you the advice you need. If so, as with your GP, try not to put too much of a burden upon them and you will doubtless find a sympathetic ear and a clear sense of how you should go forward with your problem.

Some employers, either through their occupational health services or through a welfare department, are now taking a much more helpful approach to drinking problems than used to be the case. While you may be anxious about approaching your employer, because you feel it could adversely affect your job prospects, you should not rule out the possibility. This is especially relevant if your job involves responsibility for others.

Remember, finally, that your most important resource is yourself. All the advice in this book is designed simply to assist you to accomplish one single and essential task – taking control of your own life. Other people – individuals or professional services – can be of great help and support, but in the end the person who matters most of all is yourself.